MW00883305

MONEY SHIPPING: How To Start A Profitable Amazon FBA Business In 11 Weeks

Optimize Your Profits and Go From Side Hustle to Passive Income With Minimal Effort

Cashius Lu

© **Copyright 2022 - All rights reserved.**

The content contained within this book may not be reproduced, duplicated or transmitted without direct written permission from the author or the publisher.

Under no circumstances will any blame or legal responsibility be held against the publisher, or author, for any damages, reparation, or monetary loss due to the information contained within this book, either directly or indirectly.

Legal Notice:

This book is copyright protected. It is only for personal use. You cannot amend, distribute, sell, use, quote or paraphrase any part, or the content within this book, without the consent of the author or publisher.

Disclaimer Notice:

Please note the information contained within this document is for educational and entertainment purposes only. All effort has been executed to present accurate, up to date, reliable, complete information. No warranties of any kind are declared or implied. Readers acknowledge that the author is not engaged in the rendering of legal, financial, medical or professional advice. The content within this book has been derived from various sources. Please consult a licensed professional before attempting any techniques outlined in this book.

By reading this document, the reader agrees that under no circumstances is the author responsible for any losses, direct or indirect, that are incurred as a result of the use of the information contained within this document, including, but not limited to, errors, omissions, or inaccuracies.

Table of Contents

Introduction

A big business starts small –Richard Branson

If you purchased this book, it means you have already started doing your research on how you can start an Amazon FBA business and you are looking for some help. The motivation I have behind writing this book is to provide you with as many useful tips as possible to make the process easier. I will give you an easy-to-follow roadmap that guides you through the crucial steps to starting a successful Amazon FBA business.

After reading this book, you will know exactly how the FBA industry works, what you need to focus on, and what you should avoid when running a successful e-commerce business.

You might be facing the following problems, and that is what led you to me:

- You don't know where to start with your efforts to develop an Amazon FBA business. You might also feel overwhelmed by the plethora of information and advice, and you are not sure what you can trust and what might want to prey on your hopes of building a successful business.

- You might be unhappy with your current work situation and possibly other aspects of your life. Your frustration might have grown strong, and you are thinking about this a lot and you may be wondering how you will be able to change your current situation.

- You may be struggling financially because of a low salary and no opportunity for a raise or promotion. You might have negotiated and failed, or never tried to negotiate in the first place because you are already frustrated. You might be wondering if what you have is enough to start your online business.

- You might have dreamed of having your own business, but might not have the necessary capital, time, or experience and you might be wondering if you would ever be able to start your own business.

- You might be feeling that you lack purpose in your life. You might be craving to be admired and respected by others. You might be hoping to become more acknowledged and considered a person of importance within your social circle and community by starting your own business.

Keep in mind that when you enter an Amazon FBA business, you might not start making money immediately. You need to have the right product and strategy in place if you want to reach success quickly.

Now you might be wondering how much money you can make (Connolly, 2021).

Monthly Sales	Seller Percentage
Under $500	17%
$501 - $1,000	10%
$1,001 - $5,000	17%
$5,001 - $10,000	12%
$10,001 - $25,000	16%
$25,001 - $50,000	12%
$50,001 - $100,000	8%
$100,001 - $250,000	5%
$251,000 - $500,000	1%

It's always better to have higher profit margins for your products. Many small businesses often struggle to make profits in their first year.

- More than half of all Amazon sellers make more than 10% profit.

- Around 27% of sellers see profits of more than 20%.

- Around 14% of sellers have not made any profits and 8% of sellers are unaware if they are making any profits at all (Connolly, 2021).

The following statistics show the overall lifetime profits made by sellers and the percentage of sellers who made it.

- Under $25,000 - 62%

- $25,000 - $50,000 - 6%

- $50,001 - $100,000 - 5%

- $100,001 - $500,000 - 6%

- $500,001 - $1,000,000 - 2%

- $1,000,001 - $5,000,000 - 1%

- $5,000,001 - $10,000,000 - 0%

- Not yet profitable - 9%

- Doesn't know - 9% (Connolly, 2021)

Most Amazon sellers have stated that they needed profitability within their first year of business. The following statistics show how long it took sellers to start making profits:

- Within 3 months - 22%

- Within 3-6 months - 13%

- Within 6 months to 1 year - 19%

- Within 1-2 years - 10%

- Within more than 2 years - 3%

- Doesn't know - 7% (Connolly, 2021)

So the following question you might have is how much time and money you need to invest in your Amazon business, and here are the facts:

Funds: One of the biggest hurdles many individuals face is thinking they need a lot of capital to start their Amazon business. Although this might not be the case, you should keep in mind that what you put in is what you get out. This can be in the form of time or money. Very few Amazon sellers spend more than $1,000 to start their businesses. Others put a significant amount of funding into their business, usually more than $5,000.

The funds used by sellers to start their Amazon businesses usually go towards sourcing products, paying fees to Amazon, and running promotions to attract potential buyers.

Time: The majority of Amazon sellers spend less than 20 hours a week actively working on their businesses, so it is safe to say that it is a pretty hands-free business model depending on the amount of success you want to achieve.

You will be able to just maintain your business after all the hard work of finding products, choosing your niche, and launching your product has been done.

Success Story

Neha's road to success

From a small idea to a sprawling kids' fitness brand that now delivers to over 9,000 locations across India, this is the story of Neha Sharma and the company she named Minicult.

Neha lost her job when the company she was employed with for 12 years suddenly closed down. Neha knew that there weren't a lot of options for comfortable clothing for kids, so she decided to design her own line and sell it on Amazon. Neha started her business with a spare room in her house and 50,000 rupees in her bank account. She was very excited to get her first order on the first day of launching her product. From there, Neha's business took off. She started making significant profits and put in more effort to expand her business.

About The Author

Cashius Lu is an entrepreneur and the author of Money Snacks and Money Hosts. His work is dedicated to helping readers start their own businesses in a variety of fields, securing a route to achieving passive income streams they can rely on for years to come. Cashius has started many successful businesses, favoring those that can be started as a side hustle and then scaled up to become passive income. His businesses operate in various industries, including car-sharing services, independent publishing, online retail, house-sharing services, and vending machines.

Motivation

Despite his successes, Cashius is familiar with beginner business owners 'struggles. He was once new to the game himself and is all too aware of the number of potential entrepreneurs discouraged by not knowing how to get started. He's passionate about removing the barriers to entry and helping people find their feet as they launch their careers as successful entrepreneurs. Business is Cashius 'passion, and he often has to remind himself to use his free time for other things. When he's not managing his businesses and following new ventures, he enjoys cooking, reading, and hiking.

Now that you have some basic information and can see just how profitable this business is, you can be sure that if you follow the steps I give you in this book, you will undoubtedly become successful with Amazon FBA.

By the end of this book, you should have successfully started your business, be well on your way to making great profits, and eventually feel confident enough to make this a full-time career.

So without any further delay, let's get started.

Chapter 1:

Amazon FBA: An Overview

Key Takeaway: Before we jump into how to start your business, this chapter provides an overview of everything you should know about Amazon FBA.

Amazon currently has over 6.3 million sellers in total. This should not come as a surprise because Amazon is considered to be the biggest retailer in the world. Amazon is growing in popularity, and this may make it more difficult for new sellers to become successful. But rest assured that if you choose the right niche and products, you will stand a better chance of growing your business.

If you look back at how Amazon started, you may remember that the company started by only selling books. When Amazon opened its marketplace, it started adding more products, which made them a household brand. Before Amazon launched its marketplace, it had complete control over its listings, and customers were only able to purchase what was available exclusively through Amazon.

The reason why Amazon launched its marketplace is to enable customers to have access to a wider variety of products and get everything they need in one place.

Amazon Seller Statistics

While there are a total of 6.3 million Amazon sellers registered worldwide, only about 1.5 million of those sellers are active today. Almost half of all Amazon sellers earn somewhere between $1,000 and $2,500 per month, and many sellers earn a lot more than that! (The Helium 10 Software, 2022)

Active Amazon Sellers by Country:

- United States: 1.11 Million

- United Kingdom: 281,257

- Germany: 244,425

- Italy: 216,610

- France: 211,859

- India: 205,884

- Spain: 203,413

- Japan: 173,483

- Canada: 163,595

- Mexico: 51,087

- Australia: 24,227

- UAE: 20,842

- Brazil: 15,605

- Turkey: 5,987

- Singapore: 1,721 (Chevalier, 2022)

What is Amazon FBA And How Does It Work

Amazon FBA, or Fulfillment by Amazon, was launched by Amazon to help take away some of the work from sellers. Sellers can access the massive warehouse that Amazon has available. With Amazon FBA, the work of packing and sending out orders is handled by Amazon staff.

They also handle all customer service-related inquiries, which frees up even more time for sellers. To determine whether the Amazon FBA program can add value to your online business, I would like to give you as much information as possible.

What is it?

Sellers who choose to sell their products on Amazon have two options namely; FBA (Fulfillment by Amazon) and FBM (Fulfillment by Merchant). When choosing the FBM option, you, as the seller, are responsible for packing and shipping all orders yourself. On the other hand, as mentioned above, the FBA option means that storing, packing, and shipping orders are all outsourced to Amazon.

How does it Work?

Before placing listings on Amazon, you would need to decide which fulfillment option you would prefer to use. The process of starting your Amazon FBA business is easy and straightforward. By following the steps below, you can start very soon:

1. Once you source and obtain your preferred products, you can ship them to your closest Amazon warehouse. You can get the necessary contact details and shipping address from Amazon.

2. The Amazon fulfillment center then stores your products until they receive an order. Amazon charges a storage fee depending on the size and volume of the products they have to store.

3. Amazon takes care of all transactions and once a product is shipped to a customer, they will update your inventory on your behalf.

4. Amazon packs and ships the order on your behalf.

5. Customer care and follow-ups are also handled as well as returns and refunds.

6. Profits from sales are sent to you every two weeks.

Keep in mind that you would need to follow the strict packaging guidelines that Amazon has.

Because of the hands-off approach that Amazon FBA provides, all you have to do is keep your inventory stocked and count your money.

Although the services offered by Amazon aren't free, you can rest assured that they are extremely competitive and still more affordable than handling everything yourself. Sellers are however still responsible for deciding on the right products, keeping inventory stocked up, and marketing your Amazon store to potential customers.

Inventory Fees Explained

Because Amazon stores all of your inventory, you would need to pay to store your products. This storage does come at a price, but this will depend on the volume and size of the products you are storing. Keep in mind that you might be paying more for storage during the holiday season.

Inventory stored in U.S. warehouses is charged the following month, which means that if your products are stored in March, you will only be billed between the 7th and 15th of April.

Non-dangerous goods storage fees

Month	Standard Size	Oversize
January to September	$0.75 per cubic foot	$0.48 per cubic foot

October to December	$2.40 per cubic foot	$1.20 per cubic foot

Dangerous goods storage fees

Month	Standard Size	Oversize
January to September	$0.99 per cubic foot	$0.78 per cubic foot
October to December	$3.63 per cubic foot	$2.43 per cubic foot

The reason why storage fees for dangerous goods are much higher is that these products require special storage and handling.

Should the products you store at Amazon warehouses be there for more than a year then you might be charged for long-term storage. These fees could amount to $6.90 per cubic foot or $0.15 per item that is stored (whichever is greater). This amount is then taken from your profit which is why you would need to keep track of your inventory and sales to ensure that the products you have stored are selling.

Amazon FBA: Advantages

To make an informed decision about Amazon FBA, you would need to be aware of the various advantages and disadvantages that come with the program:

Logistics support and scalability: Because of the fact that Amazon handles everything from storing to shipping your products, you can save a lot of money and, by doing so, scale your business further. Once you start selling a significant number of products, Amazon will handle the extra shipping duties, and you would just need to keep inventory levels stocked.

Fast and free shipping: When you sign up as an Amazon seller, you automatically qualify for Amazon Prime. With Amazon Prime, your products will be shipped to customers within a couple of days.

The Buy Box advantage: Professional sellers who use Amazon FBA to sell their products stand a greater chance of winning the "buy box." The buy box is an innocuous yellow button that is placed on your listing. Having this button can give you a significant boost in your sales.

Discounted shipping fees: Amazon is considered to be the king of the e-commerce world, and because of that, they have some of the largest contracts with shipping companies, which often means lower shipping costs. The wide logistics network that Amazon has can provide you with the best deals regarding shipping rates and perhaps even free shipping with Amazon Prime.

Customer support: As an Amazon FBA seller, you have access to Amazon customer support, which makes them the point of contact for customers. Amazon also handles all customer inquiries and returns with its 24/7 customer support. Keep in mind that concerning returns, there is a processing fee, but it is usually worth paying it.

Amazon FBA: Disadvantages

Along with the good comes the bad, and that's why I would like to discuss the disadvantages of Amazon FBA with you.

It's not free: Using Amazon FBA to sell your products is not free, and that is because of the storage fees that you are required to pay. Especially when you have a very low turnover, it could lead to you losing money in the long run. Even when your products are stored for longer periods, you would need to pay long-term storage fees, and removing your products from their warehouses may also come at a price. Selling smaller products with higher turnover makes Amazon FBA worth it, but it might be better if you are shipping larger products with lower turnover yourself.

Inventory management: To keep your product ranking and visibility as high as possible, you would need to regularly analyze your inventory reports. This is because you are not directly involved in the sales process, and for this reason, you would not want your products to go out of stock. Another big thing to keep in mind is Amazon's packaging and labeling guidelines. This is because Amazon may send your products back if these guidelines are not followed. You can choose to send your items yourself, use a middle-man, or have your supplier do it on your behalf, but you would need to ensure that any third party is aware of these guidelines.

Limited branding: Because your products are shipped directly from Amazon warehouses, you should know that these products are always shipped with Amazon's logo and brand name. This removes your branding opportunity because you have no control over your product packaging.

Is it Still Worth Getting Into?

In 2021, U.S. eCommerce sales surged by 14.2% from the previous year, reaching $870.8 billion. Of those sales, 41% of all transactions took place on Amazon. To put that market share dominance into perspective, the next closest competitor, Walmart, accounted for just 6% of all eCommerce sales. (Miller, 2022)

Taking the above statistics into consideration, you can see that Amazon ranks at the top of the eCommerce marketplace, not just because of its existing user base, but also because of its fulfillment services. Below are five reasons why Amazon FBA is worth every investment that you make:

Consumers Rely on eCommerce from Amazon

The shopping and searching behaviors of customers have changed dramatically since the launch of the eCommerce marketplace. This is because customers would rather turn to Amazon than Google to do their research about prices, reviews, and making purchases. This is mainly because of the convenience that Amazon provides its customers, and customers know that it is easy to find the information they are looking for on Amazon. This is made even easier when third-party sellers have excellent reviews, competitive pricing, and dependable fulfillment of their orders. Because of Amazon's ongoing growth potential, it makes sense to start a business with Amazon FBA to help increase the visibility and growth of your brand.

Fulfilled Tools and Features from Prime Aid with Quicker Delivery

With Amazon Prime, customers' orders are shipped either on the same day or within two days. The new requirements to become eligible for the Seller Fulfilled Prime (SFP) program with Amazon were put into effect on February 1, 2021. This program was put into place to help sellers provide better customer satisfaction and maintain the credibility of Amazon's eCommerce site by attracting more customers to use Amazon as their first choice of eCommerce shopping. The following tools are included in the SFP program for sellers to utilize:

Shipping Region Automation: By setting up delivery locations related to your preferred Amazon warehouse, they can set up one-day or two-day delivery, including which shipping method would be preferred.

Delivery Speed Report: As part of the FBA seller network, analytics is a valuable component. You can see which SKUs are delaying your delivery speeds and how you can speed up your delivery.

Automatic Product Classification: Depending on your product weight and dimensions, Amazon will automatically classify them as either standard or oversized.

These features are only a few of the many available on the seller dashboard to help you prevent delays and maximize delivery times. This will help with customer satisfaction, and you will also be able to see which of your products are causing delays in your delivery model and your business overall. At the end of the day, convenience is what it's all about with Amazon. You should be able to build trust with your customers through reviews and minimizing or eliminating shipping fees.

Shipping and Delivery All in One Place

With everything from shipping and delivery to a small part of marketing handled by Amazon, you can remove some of these responsibilities from your daily tasks. All of these tasks can be managed through your Amazon account, which gives you more time to focus on product creation, sourcing, inventory supply, and building your brand on other platforms.

As a new seller, selling smaller products with higher turnovers often works best. Since it will take time to build trust through customer reviews and brand recognition, it's best to stick to smaller items rather than bigger-ticket items that may be laying in the warehouse.

Amazon Seller Central will aid you in preparing your products for shipment to your preferred Amazon warehouse. This is important because every product that you ship requires a unique code, a description, and some other requirements from Amazon so your products can be tracked accurately.

Once your products are safely stored in Amazon's warehouse, they will await your first order. From there, they will take care of the packaging and shipping of your products, including customer service related to product and delivery satisfaction.

Outside Marketing is Not Required

When selling your products on your own, you might be required to do a significant amount of marketing, which could cost you a percentage of your profit. With your Amazon seller account, you can set up marketing to help you promote your products, which will ultimately help you save money. Some of these tools include:

- Sponsored products

- Sponsored brands

- Sponsored displays

- Stores

You will find that each of these has templates and widgets built in, which will help you customize your advertising and help more customers see your products. You can set up your own budget when using Amazon advertising, which includes how much you are willing to pay for ads every day. This helps you stay in control of how much you're spending every month, and you can easily view the returns you are getting on your investments.

Clear Path For Scalability

Once your business is set up and running, you should start focusing on growth. This is another reason why Amazon is perfect as long as you are using all of the tools and techniques made available to you consistently and strategically. You are also able to achieve the following with Amazon FBA:

- Promote deals and coupons

- Optimize the products you currently have available according to your analytics

- Create strategies around your brand and sales during specific seasons.

Keep in mind that, as with any other business, the work you put in will determine how fast and efficiently your business grows. You will be able to spend more time marketing your business to other potential customers once you have put all of your Amazon FBA dashboard tools to work. You will no longer have to focus on fulfillment, so you can place more time and energy on the other aspects of your business.

How Much Money Can You Make As An Amazon FBA Seller?

Every seller who signs up with Amazon FBA has a dream of becoming successful, but what does that truly mean? You might want to know how much you are truly able to make with this business model. Amazon sellers can potentially make $25,000 annually if they utilize all the tools available to them. You might not be able to make that within the first few months, but anything is possible if you have the right mindset and are willing to work towards your goals.

How Much Do Beginner Amazon Sellers Make?

The answer to this question is a bit tricky since it will depend on what products you are looking to sell and where the audience you are trying to reach is located. If I have to provide you with figures, you are looking at between $1,000 and $25,000 in sales every month, but keep in mind that sales do not always translate into profits because you would need to take your expenses into consideration.

How Long Does it Take to Become Profitable on Amazon?

It has been shown that around 64% of Amazon sellers make a profit within their first year of operation. You need to keep in mind that although Amazon is more cost-effective than running your own shop, the competition is still quite tough. Take the following statistics as an example:

- Profits within three months: 21%

- Profits within three to six months: 24%

- Profits within six months to one year: 19%

- Profits within one to two years: 11%

- Profits within more than two years: 2%

- Don't know: 5% (Omar, 2022)

Some sellers see a profit within six months, while others may take up to two years. Remember that with private label products, you might need to wait before making significant sales. This is because customers often prefer the big brands. But with the right listings, promotions, and advertising, you will start seeing a significant increase in sales on your private-label products. All you have to do is keep going.

The estimated timeline of your first few months as a seller on Amazon may look like the following:

- First week: Source products, suppliers, marketplaces, and your preferred audience.

- Next one or two weeks: Sample order for quality assurance and then waiting on arrival.

- Next four to six weeks: Build your inventory and wait on manufacturing.

- Next four weeks: Get your products shipped via sea.

- Next three to seven days: Create your listings on Amazon.

- Next one to two weeks: Launch your first products.

- Next three months: Source and market new products.

After doing all of this, you would have reached the six-month mark. Then it's time to start with the next set of tasks, which includes the following timeline:

- First 12 weeks: Get your next products ordered and wait for their samples to arrive. Then work on manufacturing, shipping, and listings.

- Next week: Launch your next set of products.

- Next six weeks: Source and market your next set of products.

Fact Box:
Throughout this chapter, I covered the following:

- What Amazon FBA business is.
- How an Amazon FBA business works.
- What are the benefits of starting an Amazon FBA business?

- What are the drawbacks of starting an Amazon FBA business?
- Why it would be worth it to start this business.
- How much you can make with your Amazon FBA business.

•

Segue: In Chapter 2, I will teach you how to register your business so you can start your Amazon FBA business.

Chapter 2:

Registering your Business

Key Takeaway: To ensure that your operation runs smoothly, it is important to set up and register your business in the most beneficial way possible.

As you start your Amazon FBA business, you should know that registering your business as an LLC is not necessary. You can start your business and trade as a sole proprietor under just your name. Although it isn't necessary, you should still consider registering your business as an LLC as you start taking your eCommerce business more seriously. You should form an LLC when:

- You are serious about growing your business and selling products on Amazon.

- You start getting more sales.

- Injuries may be caused by the use of the products you sell, including products in the sporting goods, health and wellness, and supplement niches.

- You want to separate your business and personal niches.

- You are looking for a business partner.

Registering your business as an LLC is not as difficult as you may think, and it is the best option if you are looking for long-term protection.

You might be wondering if you should get a business license to sell on Amazon, but the reality is that you don't need one, depending on your local or state government. When you are considering selling wholesale products, you might need to provide wholesalers and distributors with your documentation to show that your business is indeed legitimate.

Choosing the Right Legal Structure

Although you can start your Amazon FBA business as a sole proprietor, it may not be a sustainable solution as your business grows. So now you might be wondering which structure would be the best option for your Amazon FBA business.

Key Considerations

With all the important decisions that you need to make regarding your business, you need to choose the right business structure to register your business. When starting an online business, you need to keep product liability in mind because it could pose a big risk to the operation of your business. You might run into legal problems as you start to grow your business, which is why you need to create a legal structure to protect yourself and your business. Depending on where you are planning to sell your products, you might not fall under the list of accepted countries for Amazon seller registration. You might, however, still be able to grow your business on Amazon if you are registered as a legal entity.

Creating a legal entity for your business will not only save you time and money, but you will also be able to grow a solid business empire. So when looking at which entity might be right for your business, consider the following factors:

Ownership level: You would need to establish how involved you will be in the daily management of your Amazon business. Take the following into consideration when establishing this:

- Will you be entering into the business with other partners?

- Do you want to be involved in the daily management of the business?

- Do you want to manage the entire business by yourself?

Once you have answered these questions, you will be able to choose the right entity type that matches these purposes.

Liability protection: As an Amazon seller, you can be sued by customers. This will especially be possible when shipped products are damaged or faulty. In a situation like this, it is best to create an entity that is separate from you as the owner so you can protect your personal assets. As a business owner, your personal liabilities will be minimized. Your business liabilities will also be reduced.

Registration process: Depending on your preferences regarding the registration process, you might want to choose an LLC when structuring your business. This is because this entity type is easy and fast to incorporate. On the other hand, a corporation requires more procedures to set up.

Obligations and fees: You can minimize the cost of growing your business when you choose the right business structure. When registering your business, you will also be required to pay certain fees to the government. These fees can be for the following:

- registering your business

- getting the help of a registered agent

- annual report filing

- filing annual taxes

- annual maintenance

These fees will vary depending on the type of entity you choose to register.

Taxation: Taxes can be scary for many Amazon sellers, and even worse for beginners. Choosing the wrong entity type could lead to a higher tax burden, which will ultimately eat away at your profit. If you are required to report your taxes at the corporate tax level, then your business will have a higher tax burden. This can be detrimental to your business, especially if you are just starting to make a profit. This is because corporate taxes are nearly double that of your personal income tax rate. For this reason, you should choose a business structure that allows you to pass your company tax through your personal income tax.

Best Entity Types for Amazon FBA

Although you might think that choosing a business structure is easy, you would need to take the long-term effects into consideration before making your final decision. Below is an overview of the entity types you can choose for your business.

Limited Liability Company (LLC): An LLC is possibly the most popular option among Amazon sellers due to its simple but flexible structure. This entity can be formed with either one or more members. If you own a sole proprietorship, you are responsible for everything that goes wrong. If you own an LLC, your personal liability is limited. This means that you won't be personally liable for debts and obligations related to your business. An LLC will also protect your personal assets, as only business assets will be at risk in the event that your company is sued.

Another benefit of registering your business as an LLC is the pass-through feature related to company taxes. As mentioned earlier, this will allow you to report your income as personal income. You might also qualify for the Qualified Business Income Deduction of up to 20%. You are also able to file your taxes as a corporation, which makes it perfect for any business solution.

One disadvantage of an LLC is that it is not a structure preferred by venture capitalists. This makes it more difficult to raise the needed funds from investors. You should not be concerned about this factor as a beginner.

C Corporation: Although a C Corporation is the most common entity type in company registers, it is the least preferred type for Amazon FBA business owners. C Corporations are the most complicated entities to set up, even though they provide complete separation between your business and yourself as owner. Shareholders often own and control this entity. There are also three different tiers within this company structure, namely, shareholders, managers, and directors. The responsibility of debts and obligations is also the responsibility of the company, just like an LLC.

Taxes related to a C Corporation are submitted differently than those related to other entity types because they are submitted for company profits and cannot be included in personal taxes. The registration process for a C Corporation is also lengthier than that of an LLC because there are more procedures and documents required than when registering your business as an LLC. You would need to meet certain reporting and maintenance compliance requirements because of its complex business structure.

As a beginner Amazon seller, this might not be the perfect structure, but should you need capital funding to purchase more inventory or grow your business, you might need to consider it.

S Corporation: An S Corporation meets the Internal Revenue Code requirements and has its own distinct characteristics. An S Corporation is also owned by shareholders just like a C Corporation, but it is limited to 100 shareholders and can only have one class of stock, whereas C Corporations have no such limit. S Corporations also provide owners with personal asset protection from the creditors of the business.

Another benefit of an S Corporation is that it provides business owners with pass-through tax status, just like an LLC. This means that the profits you generate from your company will be taxed as personal income. You might also receive a deduction on the qualified business income.

You can change your business entity from a C Corporation or LLC to an S Corporation while still enjoying the pass-through tax feature. This entity is perfect, especially when you are looking to raise funds to use for your Amazon business.

Sole Proprietorship: Many beginner Amazon sellers choose to start as sole proprietors because of its simplicity. Starting as a sole proprietor means that you are the only owner and you have no separation between yourself and your business. Many Amazon sellers prefer a sole proprietorship because:

- Registration is not needed by the government.

- All profits and losses are your own.

- Tax filing is simpler than other entities.

A sole proprietorship will be your default entity as soon as you register as a seller on Amazon. You will also enjoy the Qualified Business Income Deduction if you qualify for it.

Depending on the income you can generate from your Amazon FBA business, you might be charged up to 37% in taxes if your income is over $539,900. You will also be personally liable for any debts and obligations, which could ultimately impact your personal assets if not handled properly since there would be no distinction between your business and yourself as owner.

When testing the waters on Amazon, a sole proprietorship may be perfect, but when building a brand and growing your business, registering as an LLC or corporation will become important.

Partnership: There are a handful of Amazon sellers who choose to work as a partnership. There are two different partnership structures, namely, general and limited partnerships.

- **General partnerships:** A general partnership is similar to a sole proprietorship with the exception that various individuals act as owners of the company. A general partnership in a nutshell is when two or more individuals agree to establish one account on Amazon to sell their different products in an attempt to increase sales. In other words, a general partnership is a merging of two or more sole proprietorships.

- **Limited partnerships:** This entity type is when various individuals are looking to invest in a company without having to be part of the everyday operation of the business. This partnership can consist of general and limited partners. General partners are responsible for managing the business, and they are liable for any debts and obligations. Limited partners are not involved in the everyday running of the business; they simply contribute the capital and resources needed. Taxes related to a limited partnership are handled the same as a general partnership. The one major difference is that you have to register your limited partnership with the government.

Conclusion

In summary, most Amazon sellers prefer to register their businesses as LLCs, corporations, or sole proprietorships. Concerning personal asset protection, sole proprietorships and general partnerships are not the ideal option. Defining your business needs and situation will help you make a more informed decision about the right entity structure for your business. You should also take into consideration how your business will be taxed, how many people are involved in your business, and what products you are looking to sell.

Naming Your Business

Choosing the right name for your business might not seem very important, but it could mean the difference between success and failure because it depends on how your audience relates to it. Your business identity and goals should be reflected in the name that you choose for your business. Choosing the right name before registering is also important because changing it later on could be troublesome and costly. You would need to inform the IRS when changing your business name, as well as apply for a new EIN (Employer Identification Number) and change licenses and permits.

It only takes consumers seven seconds to form a first impression of a brand, and it could take between five and seven impressions for them to remember your brand. To help your brand stick, you need to create a brand name that is catchy and memorable, not to mention evoking associations with consumers.

Why Your Business Name is Important

When choosing a business name, it is important to remember that it sets the tone for customers about what they can expect to get from you. It should also make your brand easily recognizable to potential and existing customers.

Your customers will first see your name: Potential customers will get their first impression from your business name. It will form part of the domain name as well as headline all of your advertisements. It is important to keep in mind that your business name should be search-friendly and choosing a name that is too close to your competitors or difficult to pronounce may make it hard to find. You should aim for intriguing names when choosing one for your business.

It sums up your business: The name of your business should tell your customers what you are offering and what your brand's purpose is. You should take the words that you use to describe your products into consideration, as well as the level of customer support and atmosphere that you are offering.

It shows your position in the industry: The name you choose for your business should denote trust, authority, and expertise in the industry you are operating in. You should avoid business names that may limit your growth potential.

Business Names Types

Below is an overview of the different types of business names that you may want to consider when choosing the perfect one for your business:

Descriptive names: Descriptive names are perfect for when you want to position your brand clearly to potential customers. They often tend to be functional and utilitarian, and misinterpretation is less likely. You may, however, not be able to tell a story with a descriptive name, and it may also take away personality, but you can benefit from it when entering a new market. Keep in mind that you might find it difficult to trademark your business when your name contains real words.

Suggestive names: Customers should have feelings evoked when using your products or services, especially when you are using emotive brand names. Connotations within suggestive names are used in an attempt to convey the experience related to the brand. If your business is focused on more than just the products or services that you are offering, then creative names will work great for your business. You will also be able to trademark suggestive names easier than descriptive ones because they are often original.

Arbitrary names: To embody a brand's personality, many individuals will use words derived from Latin, Greek, or other foreign roots and then modify them. These names are often fun and memorable, and they often don't have any reference to the actual operation of the company. Although I should mention that when customers repeat the name enough, they will start to associate it with the specific product or service that the company is offering. (Think Nike!)

Acronyms/initialisms: When choosing a long name for your company, you might think it's wiser to use acronyms to shorten it, but in reality, they lack meaning, emotion, and imagery. Take BMW as an example; it's an acronym for Berlin Motor Works, but no one will know that because they have always referred to their vehicle as a BMW. Acronyms may make it more difficult for customers to remember your company name, and you will also have a harder time trademarking your business. Using acronyms as a business name in the e-commerce industry is not recommended.

Names from other languages: This is when you are using words found in other languages and using their connotations.

How to Name Your Business

When choosing a name for your business, it's a good idea to first make a list of potential names. You should do sufficient market research, talk to customers, and get feedback from family and friends until you find a name that you are happy with.

Brainstorm: You should compile a comprehensive list of potential names for your business by using various brainstorming techniques. Take a look at other companies in your industry and what their names are. Think about how they came up with their names, and if the industry has a naming convention that they prefer. You can also think about some local brands and what they make you think about when you hear their names. Ensure that you are using all of the feedback you are receiving before going public with your business.

- **Word dump:** Think about words that may relate to your business and start writing them down. Don't overthink this step, this is all about creating something that you can start to work with. You can set a timer for yourself in this step, and you should stop when the timer goes off. Write down everything you think of without thinking about it twice.

- **Thesaurus:** You can then use a thesaurus to check the words you have written down, and find synonyms and antonyms for these words. This will help you create an even more detailed list of words that you can use to choose your business name. You should also use this step to eliminate any words that you no longer feel work with your brand.

- **Name Generator:** By simply adding a few keywords to a name generator website, you will be able to find tons of potential business names. Most of these sites also check domain availability so you can choose a name that you can easily register as a ".com." You should specify the industry you are working in, the products and services you are offering, and any other filters that you might find relevant to your business. The more information you add to your search the better chance you will have of finding the right name for your business.

List business names: Once you have created a word dump and come up with potential names for your business, you can now go through and choose names that you think would work best for your business. You can start eliminating names that you think won't work and keep the ones that best describe your business. You need to be careful of names that sound too much like those of other businesses, or they could hold you liable for trademark violations. To shortlist names for your business, you should take the following into consideration:

- **Does it make sense:** The name that you choose for your business should make your target audience feel like they have chosen the right business. If your business is targeting a younger audience then you might want to stay away from a name that could make you sound like a law firm.

- **Does it have meaning:** If your name has an interesting or intriguing backstory then the opportunity for your audience to connect with it will be greater. There are brand names that are derived from ancient mythology that have seen great success over the past couple of years, for example, "Nike" and "LEGO."

- **Will it be remembered:** One thing to keep in mind when you name your business is the ability for your audience to remember it. If the name you choose has no relation to your brand or if it is too long it might slip your audience's mind and they will forget it quickly.

- **Is it easy to spell:** Keeping search engines in mind when naming your business is important because your audience will want to look you up. When your audience misspells your name they may fail to find you if the name is too hard to spell.

- **Is it good looking:** Your logo, marketing material, social media accounts, and other materials will all contain your business name. This is why it is important to make your business name appealing and pleasantly sounding when it is said out loud. You should take into consideration the shapes of your letters and how they will look on your logo.

Follow the naming rules: Another important consideration to keep in mind is the restrictions your state may have on business names. You should always check with your local business bureau to ensure that your name is acceptable. You may be able to register your business under one name, while you may have multiple trading names for your business. You should also take into consideration the type of entity you are looking to form, as you would need to add the necessary information at the end of your business name, for example:

- LLC: Should include Limited Liability Company or LLC at the end.

- C-Corporations: Should include Corporation, Incorporated, Company, or

Limited or the abbreviations Corp., Inc., Co., or Ltd.

- Informal business structures: These businesses often have limited rules, but you should still take your name into careful consideration.

- Sole proprietor: You may be able to operate under your name or a fictitious name when opening a sole proprietor company.

Check availability: You should always be cautious and check if your chosen business name has not already been taken by another company. You can do this by checking domain availability. Keep in mind that domain names with a .com at the end are often trusted more than ones registered with a .org or .net.

Register Your Business Name

To register your business, you would need to approach your district legal entity. You might also want to get in touch with the United States Patent and Trademark Office if you are looking to trademark your business. You would also need to register your business with the secretary of state's office, a business bureau, or a business agency if you are looking to register your business as an LLC, C-corp, partnership, or nonprofit organization.

Registering Your Business

How to Register a Business in the US in Six Steps

Registering your business in the U.S. may seem like a daunting task, but it is simple if you follow the steps laid out below.

Step 1: Choosing your Legal Business Structure

As mentioned earlier in this chapter, it is necessary to choose the right legal business structure for your business before registering it. You would need to make sure that the structure you choose suits the needs of your business. This first step will help set the tone for your business, including how you file taxes and what your operations will look like on a daily basis.

Step 2: Decide on your location

Your business location is where you will be operating. Since you will be starting an online Amazon FBA business, you might only add an address for correspondence and tax purposes. You might not need to register your business in the state where you are residing if you have an ecommerce business. You might even be able to register your business in a state that has no state taxes if you have access to an address in that state.

Step 3: Decide on your business name

When registering your business, you need to have a business name. You should follow the steps provided previously to ensure that your business name is as unique as possible.

Step 4: Apply for a federal tax number

When registering a company, you need to do so on a state and federal level to ensure that it is a legal entity. To register your business on a federal level you need to apply for a federal tax number or employer identification number (EIN), which acts like a social security number for your business. This number will allow you to submit your tax forms and other paperwork to both the federal and state governments.

Step 5: Get the necessary licenses and permits

To trade legally, you need to ensure that you have the necessary licenses and permits to do so. These may differ at the state and federal levels, and you can use the Small Business Administration website to check whether you need certain licenses or permits to operate within your chosen industry. Checking to see what your company needs concerning licenses and permits could help prevent costly fines and avoid putting your business at risk.

Step 6: Open a business bank account

Depending on the type of legal structure you are using to open your business, you would need to open a business bank account to separate your business and personal income and assets from each other. To do so, you would need to complete your business registration, as you will need the registration documents to prove that you are a legitimate business owner. Keep in mind that some banks would require an in-person visit, so you might want to choose a bank you can easily go to.

Taxes to Be Aware of

Taxes can be a daunting topic for many individuals, and for that reason, I have put together some helpful tips to ensure that your business is ready for anything:

Should I Get An Accountant?

The short answer to this question is yes. This is because a professional accountant can not only help you save money on your taxes but may also be able to turn the taxes you owe into a tax refund for your business.

What is a 1099-K Form?

This form is issued by Amazon to show the IRS what your annual and monthly gross sales were, and it will also include sales tax and shipping fees. This form is often filled in on your behalf by Amazon, so you would not need to do anything. They will also send it to both you and the IRS, as long as the requirements are met.

Who Gets a 1099-K Form on Amazon?

To obtain a 1099-K form from Amazon, you would need to have made $20,000 in sales and have 200 individual transactions on your account. This means that not all sellers will get a 1099-K form from Amazon. You would need to provide Amazon with your tax status if you have at least 50 transactions on your account; otherwise, you might not be able to perform any transactions on the platform. You can do this under the tax information tab on your seller central account.

Where Can I Get My 1099-K Form?

Amazon emails the 1099-K forms to active Amazon sellers, but if you have not received yours, then you can follow the steps below to get it:

- Log into your Amazon Seller Central Account.

- Go to the reports menu.

- Go to the Tax Document library.

- Click on download/print for your 1099-k form for the year.

What If My 1099-K Form is Inaccurate or I Didn't Receive One?

You can contact seller support if you have not received your 1099-K form, and should you find mistakes on your report, you can follow the steps below to get them fixed:

- Ensure that you are reporting any unadjusted total gross sales. These are based on shipping dates and not sales dates. Keep in mind that orders that were shipped in January will not show on your report.

- You would need to print a date range report by following the steps below:

  - Go to your Seller Central and select the reports tab.

  - Click on the *Date range reports*.

  - Select the *Generate a statement* tab.

  - When the *Generate Date Range Report* pops up, you can do the following:

    - Select the *Summary* option.

- You can then choose between *monthly* or *custom* and insert the date you are looking for.

- Click the *Generate* button.

- Once you have your report generated you can review it under the *Data Range Report* tab.

- You should then calculate your adjusted gross sales by adding up all the amounts in the reports columns together.

Do I Need a Business License To Be An Amazon FBA Seller?

The short answer is no, unless your state requires that you have one. If your Amazon FBA business has an office, employees, and large expenses, then it might be a good idea to apply for a business license. Most Amazon FBA business owners register their businesses as LLCs because it gives them protection from taking personal responsibility should their company run into any issues and is better concerning taxes.

Do I Need to File A Form 1040 When I Have A Business License?

When operating a business in your state, you are required to file Form 1040 or Schedule C. Using an accountant or bookkeeping software like Quickbooks is the best way to do so because you would need to keep track of your expenses during the year of filing.

What is Sales Tax?

Products considered to be non-essential are subject to sales tax in the United States. This does, however, vary from state to state. It may become difficult to keep track of sales taxes when you are selling across various states, which is why it is better to obtain an accountant to assist you with your business accounting.

What Is A Sales Tax Nexus?

The sales tax nexus is where your business has a physical presence. This means that if you have products in two different states, you would need to collect sales taxes from both states. You would need to contact an accountant to find out if you would need to collect and remit sales taxes for the state where your business is located.

When Do I Need To File Sales Tax?

You should apply for a sales tax permit when you are looking to collect sales tax. You will be instructed when to file your taxes once your application has been reviewed. You will have to file either monthly, quarterly, or annually, depending on the state in which you are filing. You should take note of the due dates that are being given to you because should you fail to do so it might result in the termination of your sales tax permit.

What's a Deductible?

Deductibles are expenses within your business that you can write off. Subtracting the costs of running your business from your gross income will help you lower the taxes that you would need to pay. This can help you save money for your business and your taxes.

What's Deductible?

Below are some of the things you can write off as deductions:

- cost of goods sold

- costs of shipping

- costs for your home office

- amazon fees

- mileage

- donations

- subscriptions

- education

- software used for keeping track of taxes and inventory

- advertising your business online

- salaries and benefits paid to employees

- fees paid to consultants

Fact Box:
Throughout this chapter, I covered the following:

- How you can choose the right legal structure for your business.
- What the best structure is for your business.
- Why it's important to give your business a name.
- The various types of business names.
- How to choose the best name for your business.
- How to register your business in the U.S.
- Do you need an accountant and when should you get one?
- What a 1099-K form is.
- Where you can find your form.
- What to do when your 1099-K form is not accurate.
- Whether you should file a schedule C form for your licensed business.
- What sales taxes are.
- When you should file your sales tax.
- What a deductible is and if you can use it.

Segue: In the next chapter, you will learn about how you can sign up for Amazon FBA and how you should set up your account.

Chapter 3:

Signing up with Amazon FBA

Key Takeaway: The signup process for Amazon FBA is rather easy; however, there are some things new sellers should be aware of when setting up their accounts.

With the launch of fulfillment by Amazon, sellers have been provided with more customer service infrastructure and fulfillment options. It also gives customers more options regarding shipping. Amazon FBA is designed to hold and ship products on behalf of the third-party seller; they also handle all customer service-related queries on behalf of the seller. For a fee, anyone is able to utilize Amazon FBA to hold and distribute orders, which takes the hassle away from sellers having to store and fulfill orders themselves. Not to mention not dealing with customer service.

Brad Stone said the following in his book, *The Everything Store*:

"Bezos and his lieutenants sketched their own virtuous cycle, which they believed powered their business. It went something like this: Lower prices led to more customer visits. More customers increased the volume of sales and attracted more commission-paying third-party sellers to the site. That allowed Amazon to get more out of fixed costs like the fulfillment centers and the servers needed to run the website. The greater efficiency then enabled it to lower prices further. Feed any part of this flywheel, they reasoned, and it should accelerate the loop."

Amazon made various other improvements to ensure that:

- Customers find the site more attractive and convenient when buying on Amazon.

- Sellers find it easier to sell their products on Amazon.

This allowed Amazon to feed the flywheel, which aided it in spinning faster. By establishing FBA, sellers are able to establish and grow their business without having to worry about the logistics

"Last year, Amazon accounted for 49% of all global online shopping traffic. Of all shopping done online, worldwide, fully half of it was done on Amazon" (McDaniel, 2022).

What Every Seller Should Know Before They Start

Amazon has revolutionized the e-commerce world with its large customer base, and it is one of the largest e-commerce websites today. But this does not come for free, and Amazon charges their sellers several different fees that you would need to be aware of and prepared for. These fees collected by Amazon are used to pay their employees and keep their operations running smoothly. Before becoming an Amazon seller, you would need to meet certain requirements, regulations, and fees regarding Amazon's online rules. This may leave sellers with a lot of questions, and I would like to answer some of those questions below.

Customer-Centric eCommerce Platform

Amazon has dedicated its time and energy to making its site as customer friendly as possible by supplying them with as many products as possible. The one main attraction for consumers is Amazon's free and fast shipping, especially when using an Amazon Prime membership. Amazon takes customer service very seriously because they understand that customers are what give value to the company. This means that all measures are put in place to work in the customer's favor. All policies and changes that are made by Amazon will not necessarily be beneficial to you as the seller, but they are there to protect shoppers and provide them with the best shopping experience possible.

Four Ways To Sell Products On Amazon FBA

The four main ways that you can sell products on Amazon are retail arbitrage, wholesale, private label, and passion products. Each of these has its benefits and drawbacks.

Retail arbitrage is the practice of buying products from retail stores at a cheaper rate and then selling them at a higher price on Amazon.

Amazon wholesale is where you, as the seller, buy products in bulk at a discounted rate and then sell them at retail price or more. Private labeling is the practice of putting your own brand on products that you buy from a manufacturer and then selling them on Amazon. Unique items are items that have not been previously sold and are unique on the market.

When looking closer at the various strategies mentioned above, I found the following. Retail arbitrage is profitable depending on the price of products in retail stores. You will also be competing with other sellers who are buying the same products and selling them on the marketplace. Wholesalers and private labels have the same problem, which is that other sellers might get in contact with the same manufacturer that you are working with, which may mean more competition. Unique items may have less competition than the other strategies, but you would need to work harder to advertise your products, and you might not get as much interest as you would have wished for.

Knowing the different strategies is important before picking your niche because the decision you make could mean major profits or major losses, so choosing wisely is important.

Fees, Fees, Fees (And Lots of it)

It's a fact that convenience comes with a price, and many new sellers on Amazon FBA are not prepared for the number of fees that they would need to pay. Some of the fees that you, as a seller, are responsible for when selling on Amazon include:

- FBA fulfillment fees

- monthly inventory storage fees

- removal and disposal order fees

- special handling fees

- return processing fees

These are just some of the fees that need to be paid along with your selling plan and fees related to referrals. Because of this, many sellers underestimate the costs related to starting their FBA business. If you believe that the product you are looking to sell will be loved by individuals, then you might want to take a chance at raising funds for your business through one of the crowdfunding platforms that are being established to help sellers start their FBA business.

Keep Inventory Stocked Up

Although you can have your inventory sent directly to Amazon from the manufacturer, it might be better to first have products sent to you in order to perform quality assurance. This will help you ensure that your products are without fault, won't need any alterations, and that labels are properly placed before products are shipped to fulfillment centers.

There are essentially seven steps that you should follow when sending your products to the fulfillment center, and these can be found in your Seller Central account. These steps are put into place to systematize how you move your inventory between yourself or your manufacturer to an Amazon fulfillment center.

In order to send your inventory, you can follow these steps:

- Click on the *Manage Inventory* tab.

- Select the products you would like to stock up on.

- Click on *Action on selected*.

- Then click on *Send/replenish Inventory*.

- Then you want to create a new Shipping plan.

- Finally, you would need to complete all the technical details of your product in your shipping plan, which is explained by Amazon on the Seller Central website.

Scaling Your Amazon Store With FBA

Amazon FBA is a great place to scale your business because as long as you are not selling hazardous or perishable products, you can store as much inventory as you like. This is why Amazon is such a great side hustle for many individuals. They can do what they want and work from where they want with a hands-off approach to the logistics of an Amazon business. This means that Amazon sellers have freedom regarding their business, and they have more time to spend with their families and take on other things they are passionate about.

Create Your Account

"In 2022, 63% of consumers started their shopping searches on Amazon, with low product prices, free or low-cost shipping, and convenience as the reason they chose to shop online instead of in-store. More than half of consumers shopped on Amazon weekly or more, and towards the end of the year, 67% of consumers chose to shop on Amazon for holiday gifts."

According to the information provided above, it is proven that Amazon is showing enormous growth potential for individuals. But you should keep in mind that you would still need to go through the registration process with Amazon to become an official seller.

Creating a Seller Account on Amazon

Once you have completed all the steps mentioned above, you are ready to start setting up your Amazon seller account. Below are steps that you should follow so you can set up your account quickly and easily:

Step 1: Go to https://sell.amazon.com

Step 2: Go to the pricing tab

You can compare the selling plans that Amazon has to offer by clicking on the *Compare selling plans* tab under the pricing section. This will take you to the comparison page, where you will be able to view the difference between individual and professional seller accounts. Keep in mind that when you skip directly to *sign up*, you will be taken to the professional seller registration page, whereas the *see pricing* link will give you the option to choose between individual and professional registrations.

Step 3: Decide between a professional or individuals seller account

Signing up as a professional is better when you are aiming to sell more than 40 products per month. This plan will also help you save money even if you are just selling on Amazon as a side hustle. If you want to sell on a smaller scale, you can choose the individual plan.

One thing to keep in mind is that your products will not be eligible for the buy box when you choose the individual plan, and you will not be able to advertise your products on Amazon.

Step 4: Add your email and click on *Create a New Account*

Once you have chosen your preferred seller plan, you will be taken to a window that will require you to add your email address and password to open your seller account. Once you have entered this information, you can click on *Next* to be taken to the following window.

Here, you will be asked to enter a verification code that was sent to your preferred email address. This will allow Amazon to verify that your email address is valid. Once this step is done, you will be redirected to a new page. You will need the following documentation and information to complete your registration, but Amazon will let you know:

- valid government-issued ID or password

- recent bank account or credit card statement

- chargeable credit card

- mobile phone number

Step 5: Enter your business location and type

You should share the following information with Amazon to complete your registration:

- **Business Location:** This will be the country that you are looking to operate from. You should ensure that this is accurate as Amazon will be verifying it.

- **Business type:** You will need to choose the type of business you will be operating as. Amazon has the following types that you can choose from:

  - state-owned business

  - publicly-owned business

  - privately-owned business

  - charity

  - No, I am an individual.

  You would want to choose the last option if you have not formed an entity for your business at the time of registration. You would need to enter your full name in the next step if you choose this option.

- **Your full name:** When Amazon asks you to enter your full name you would need to add your name as per your ID document which should include your first, middle, and last name.

After all the necessary information has been entered, you will be able to click *Agree and continue* to move to the next step.

Step 6: Personal information

During this step, you would need to provide Amazon with some of your personal information. This will include a copy of your identification, which can either be your passport number or your driver's license. You should also verify your phone number through a text message or phone call. Your number will be verified once you enter the pin you received from Amazon. You should ensure that all the information you entered is correct before you are able to move on to the next step of your application. Once this is done, you should click on the *next* button to move on to the next step of your application.

Step 7: Billing information

In this step, you will be asked to provide your bank account number and credit card number so Amazon can have access to your billing information. You should again ensure that the information you entered is correct to avoid any delays in your application.

Step 8: Product and Amazon store information

Once your credit card information has been entered and verified, you will be asked various questions regarding your Amazon store and the products you are planning to sell. You would need to answer the following questions in order to move on to the next step:

- What is the name of your Amazon store?

- Do you have UPC codes for your products?

- Do you have any diversity certifications?

- Are you the manufacturer or brand owner of the products you are planning to sell? Should you answer yes to this question you would be asked if you own the government-registered trademark for the product.

Once you are done with this process, you can click the *next* button to move on to the next step in your registration.

Step 9: Verification of your identity

During this stage, you would need to upload an image of your ID and your bank statement for

Amazon to verify your identity. You should click the submit button once these copies have been uploaded. You will then receive a video call from an Amazon associate to complete your identity verification. This is to ensure that all your documents and personal information are indeed correct.

Once this step is done, you have completed your registration, and you can start selling on Amazon. To protect yourself, I recommend that you set up two-step verification on your account.

The Amazon Checklist

To completely and successfully complete your registration to become an Amazon seller, you need to ensure that all the necessary information is readily available. For that reason, I am providing you with a checklist that you can use when registering:

Business Info

All of the relevant business information related to your Amazon business would need to be entered upon registration. This includes the legal name of your business, your business address, and all the contact information of your business.

Email Address

You would need to have a registered email address for an individual company account. This should be set up before you start your registration process because you will be receiving emails from Amazon during your registration.

Credit Card

You would need an internationally chargeable credit card with a valid billing address. This credit card number will be added to your profile; if this credit card number is not valid, then your registration may be canceled.

Phone Number

The phone number that you provide Amazon with should be working because you will be contacted by Amazon to complete your registration.

Tax ID

You will be requested to add your Social Security number or company's Federal Tax ID number during the registration process. Once one of these numbers has been submitted, you will be directed to a 1099-K Tax Document Interview page.

State Tax ID

Should you reside in a state where you have a tax nexus, you would need to enter your state tax ID information. You should consult with a tax attorney or tax accountant specializing in this so you can be provided with the most recent Amazon tax nexus information.

Fact Box:
Throughout this chapter, I covered the following:

- What you should know about starting your Amazon FBA business.
- What fees are related to this business model?
- How you are able to better scale your business.
- Creating your seller account on Amazon.
- A complete checklist to start your Amazon FBA business.

Segue: In Chapter 4, I will help you decide on the right niche and the right products for your business.

Chapter 4:

Finding the Right products

Key Takeaway: Finding profitable products is an art. But with the right mindset and tools, you'll be able to find the best niches and products for your Amazon FBA business.

Amazon FBA does not have a minimum requirement, and you can sell your product in single units if needed. Keep in mind that there is a minimum limit for when you restock your products in your Amazon store. By improving your inventory performance index (IPI) score, you will be able to increase the storage limit you have access to. This is so Amazon can ensure your products are selling, and you won't be sitting with unsold inventory. Your IPI score can be tracked on your inventory dashboard.

Popular Product Categories on Amazon

Books

Books have become increasingly popular over the past decade. Books are how Amazon started, and since then, it has become a popular niche for many sellers. To make this a profitable venture, you can look at picking up books for one dollar and then selling them for 10 times their original price.

Things for Babies

As long as the population keeps growing and more and more babies are being born every day, baby items will always stay in demand. Since babies don't stay the same size they require various things throughout their lives. Baby items are also inexpensive to get a hold of, it is lightweight and durable, and many individuals are always looking for them.

Gold and Gems

Jewelry is and will always be in demand. Keep in mind that you would need to advertise your products properly because there is huge competition in the jewelry market. Although the profit margins for jewelry are high, you should take advantage of long-tail keywords that are unique to your product. If you are intending to use single keywords to describe your products, then you might as well quit before you get started; there is too much competition in the jewelry market.

Exercise Clothing

With more and more people realizing that exercise is needed to live a healthy lifestyle, the clothing industry and especially exercising items have started to skyrocket. Amazon has seen an increase in sales in this niche over the past few years. This makes it a perfect niche to enter, especially if you are offering new items—people will not be interested in purchasing second-hand exercise items. This will also allow you to increase your profitability even more.

Electronic Items

Tech items are not only high niche items, but they also provide you as a seller with a few additional benefits, including:

- lower commission fees from Amazon

- various choices and subsets under each category

- various new items becoming available

- different advertising styles for your audiences depend on the brand name you are trying to sell... although most of these items do the same thing

- retail arbitrage—lots of opportunities here

The Most Successful Products on Amazon

The following section will only serve as a guide to show you the most profitable products currently available on Amazon. You will still need to look at the market to make sure that the product you choose will still be in demand by the time you get access to it and advertise it on your Amazon store.

Amazon Best Sellers for 2022

The following categories currently have the highest sales potential on Amazon:

- toys and games

- electronics

- camera and photo equipment

- video games

- books

- clothing, shoes, and jewelry

- handmade items

- pet supplies

- home and kitchen products

Categories like CD and vinyl should preferably be avoided due to streaming services taking over the music world, which causes sales of these products to drop.

How to Select the Best Products for Your Shop

The following tips will help you scale your business, but that does not mean that every product you choose to sell will be successful. You should keep Amazon's fees and guidelines in mind when choosing a product as they would need to meet these protocols while still providing you with a profit. Using the tips set out below you will save a lot of time while seeing how your business grows:

High Product Value

When choosing products to sell on Amazon, you would need to look for products that you can easily write off. The chances of at least one customer returning a product are always there, and you would not want to sit with something that is damaged. Products that you are looking to sell should be priced between $10 and $100, and the profit that you place on these products should be at least half of that value. This will protect you against bankruptcy should a product be returned because of damages or any other reason.

Target Impulse Buys

When choosing the right product, you should keep the price in mind. Many consumers will see a product priced over $100 as an investment, and this will lead them to do their research on the product, your company, reviews, and debate the purchase. By the time this is all done, they might have changed their minds about the purchase, which will lead to you losing a sale. Consumers are more than likely able to justify a purchase of $25 to $40, and they will not spend as much time on research. This will increase your sales and lead to your products selling out faster.

The Smaller the Better

Another consideration to keep in mind when choosing the product you want to sell on your Amazon store is the size of the product. The bigger the product is, the more you will need to pay in fees. This is because the pricing model of Amazon is based on product size and weight. To increase your profits, it is recommended that you stick to smaller products that are lighter in weight to minimize the fees charged by Amazon.

Amazon Best Seller Rank

To help you choose the right product for your store, Amazon has tools that will help you out. The best seller rank (BSR) is the perfect tool to help you establish which products are currently selling exceptionally well on the site. It also breaks down the categories and subcategories to show how they are performing in each. As a general rule, you should preferably choose products in the top 5000 BSR. These are often the products that sell more than a few units per day and are considered profitable. You should always ensure that your products are moving, especially when you have invested funds in your Amazon FBA business.

Avoid Restricted Brands

Although certain brands may be very popular on Amazon, they don't allow sellers to sell them. One of these brands is Apple. These brands are classified by Amazon as restricted brands. These are restricted for various reasons, including that these companies have dealt with Amazon, which means that they have the authorization to sell these products. Some other brands may be knockoffs or fake versions of the original, and Amazon has a zero-tolerance policy on these products.

Although Amazon has not published an extensive list of the restricted brands, it's safe to assume that if a brand is popular, you should stay clear of selling them on Amazon. Gucci, Bose, American Girl, and KitchenAid are just a few of the restricted brands.

You should always keep profit in mind when choosing a product to sell on Amazon. The costs related to a product could include the manufacturing of the product, the storage and shipping costs related to the product, how well you expect it to sell, and the overall product value. Once you have considered all these costs, your product should thrive in your Amazon store.

Fact Box:
Throughout this chapter, I covered the following:
- The most popular product categories on Amazon.
- The best-selling products trending right now.
- What to look out for when choosing your products.
- What you should avoid when choosing your products.

- Best seller rank on Amazon.

Segue: Chapter 5 will be covering some helpful tips and tricks on how you will be able to be successful as an FBA drop shipper.

Drum Up Some Healthy

Competition

No competition, no progress. –Bela Karolyi

As you amass the knowledge you need to start a successful Amazon FBA business, it might feel counterintuitive to share the information with would-be competitors... But did you know that competition is good for business?

The simplest reason for this is that it provides reassurance: If you're up against healthy competition, you know that your customers are returning because you're doing something right, and that tells you to keep on your trajectory. It also means that your business has distinct qualities that separate it from the rest... and if it doesn't, you'll know you're losing business to someone else, and you'll be able to take steps to rectify that.

When you can identify your business 'individual traits, you'll be able to market it more effectively and reel in new customers. In turn, the more your customers continue to choose you, the better you'll serve them, creating customer loyalty and a positive feedback loop that will serve your business well.

So with all that in mind, I'd like to ask you to stir up that competition a little and show other people with the seed of a business idea what they can do to get started with Amazon FBA. Don't worry—it's the easiest thing you'll have to do as your own idea starts to blossom... All you need to do is leave a short review.

By leaving a review of this book on Amazon, you'll show other potential business owners where they can find the information they need to get their Amazon FBA idea off the ground.

Simply by letting other readers know how this book has helped you and what they'll find inside, you'll point them toward the information they're looking for.

Thank you for your support. We all need help when we're first starting out... and a bit of healthy competition is only going to be a good thing for the Amazon FBA industry.

>>> **Click here to leave your review on Amazon.**

Chapter 5:

Creating Listings

Key Takeaway: The ability to create captivating things is crucial for a successful vendor on Amazon.

Emily Dayton explains the following statistics on her bigcommers.com website:

- Each month more than 197 million people around the world get on their devices and visit Amazon.com.

- Amazon's share of the U.S. eCommerce market hit 49%. That's 5% of all retail spending across the entire country.

- Nine out of 10 consumers price-check products on Amazon.

- Two percent of Echo owners have purchased a product via Alexa.

- Amazon sells over 1.1 million home improvement products.

- 95 million people have Amazon Prime memberships in the U.S.

- $1,400 is the average spent by Amazon prime members each year.

- FBA gives sellers a 30% - 50% increase in sales.

- Amazon shipped over 5 billion items worldwide in 2017.

- More than 50% of all Amazon sales come from third-party sellers.

- 80% of sellers also sell on other platforms outside of Amazon (Dayton, 2019).

What are Amazon Product Listings?

An Amazon product listing is a page for every product you have on your Amazon store that displays all the information related to your product. This information includes your product title, images, description, and the price you are selling your product for. This page is often used by consumers before making a purchase so they can see what the product is about and then add it to their cart. This means that you would need to ensure your product listing is perfect to make sales and reach success with your business.

What it Does

There are two main functions of your Amazon product listing, which include:

- enabling your products to be found on searches

- telling consumers to purchase your products

This is why it is important to optimize your product listing on your Amazon storefront.

Essential Elements

Product Title: When writing your Amazon product listing, you will have up to 500 characters to describe your product in detail. Some products, however, will only allow you 250 characters. This will allow you to give as much detail about your product as possible. Your title essentially gives you the opportunity to give a mini description of the product you are listing.

You should aim to go into as much detail as possible when writing your product title. Adding a main keyword to your title is also essential because it will allow your product to come up in Amazon searches. Adding your product name, brand, model number, color, size, type, and any other necessary information is also important to increase your product's attractiveness.

Images: When creating your product listing, you should add at least five images. These images should show the size of your product as well as how the product is used. You should aim to include images that show multiple angles as well as what the product looks like in its packaging. Keep Amazon requirements in mind when adding images to your listing.

Bullet points: You are allowed to add seven bullet points to your products, right under your price, product options, and shipping details. In this section, it is recommended that you list all the main features and benefits of your product to convince consumers to purchase it. Adding secondary keywords in this section will also increase the chances of your products popping up in Amazon searches. The bullet points are located right above the fold and close to the images, price, and *Add to Cart* button, which puts them in an ideal position and makes them essentially more important than your product description.

Description: Your product description may not be as important as your bullet points, but don't think that it is not important at all. The description of your product will provide more information about it and will also include some main keywords. Keeping your customer in mind when writing your product description is important. You should know what customers want to know about your product and add that to your description.

How to Create a Listing

Storefronts in a shopping mall are what give customers the initial impression of a business and what convinces them to make a purchase or not. With an Amazon FBA business, you should think of your product listing as being your storefront. Your Amazon listing is what will attract customers, and what you add to your listing is what will convince them to make a purchase. customers get their first impression of your storefront with the detailed description, customer reviews, and added images you provide.

To make sales on Amazon, it is important to give buyers the necessary knowledge. This knowledge will allow customers to make an informed decision when making a purchase. This is why it is important to craft your product listing in a way that will attract customers quickly and easily. To help you do this, I will provide you with a few valuable tips below. These tips will include identifying some of the key elements of your product page so you can attract more customers and increase your sales, so let's get started:

How to Set Up Your Listing

Should you be the first seller to offer a specific product, you would need to create a new listing. On the other hand, if there are multiple sellers offering the same product, you might share a listing on Amazon.

When creating a unique listing, you should log into your Seller Central dashboard and go to the *Inventory* option under your menu. You should then select the *Add a Product* option under the dropdown menu.

A new page will open up where you need to choose between an existing product or making your own listing. You can select *Create a new listing* when setting up a listing for a unique product.

The following section will give you the option to choose the category and subcategory under which your product will fall. Once you have chosen your options, you need to add the necessary information about your product. The information you add should be both informative and engaging, so you can build trust with your buyers and help them understand why they should buy your products.

Elements of a Great Product Listing

When creating your Amazon product listing, you should keep keywords in mind so you can place your product at the top of search results. Another essential element in driving customers to purchase your items is to include captivating copies and images. The following basic elements are essential to a great Amazon listing:

- keywords that are SEO-driven

- descriptions that are detailed

- formatting that is scannable

- visuals that are engaging

If you create your listing with these elements in mind, you will be sure to increase your product sales.

Keywords that are SEO-driven

SEO or Search Engine Optimization is what drives customers to your listings. It helps search engines place your products high in search results and makes your products more visible to buyers. The keywords you use are interpreted by both Amazon and outside search engines to establish if your product is relevant to specific search results. You need to add keywords that are regularly used by your targeted audience so your listing can be ranked high where it matters.

There are many resources available that you can use to choose the right keywords to add to your product listings. Keep in mind that some search engines will penalize you if you practice keyword stuffing. Keywords should not be non-helpful or out-of-context as many search engines will be able to detect them.

Moderately adding keywords to your listings is recommended to avoid lower rankings. Below are a few tips that you can use:

- **Include target keywords:** When creating your product, the title only uses the necessary keyword phrases. Adding too many keywords will make your listing look like spam to search engines and customers.

- **Distribute your keywords evenly:** It is recommended that you add the most important keywords at the most two to three times throughout your listing and keep them spread out to every 100–200 words if possible.

- **Use variations:** Changing up the way you are using your keywords will also increase your chances of popping up in search results, for example, instead of just using "purple phone case" you can also use "phone cases that are purple" and "purple-colored phone cases."

Descriptions That are Detailed

The description that you add to your product will essentially act as the salesman on the shop floor.

It will help gain customer trust and increase curiosity and interest among customers.

The description that you write should be accurate and comprehensive and should not include any false promises. False promises may gain you a few initial sales, but if your product does not live up to these promises, it may lead to returns and harm your reputation. Your ODR, or order defect rate, can be increased if a buyer decides to file an Amazon A-to-Z guarantee claim, which is completed when a product does not match its description.

Buyer motivations should also be included in a great listing description. You should highlight the benefits that your item has that customers will actually care about. If your product description contains all the necessary information then customers won't glaze over it. Readers will often think about how a specific product will improve their lives and this will increase the likelihood of a customer purchasing it.

Formatting that is scalable

The likelihood of a customer reading your entire listing is very small, that's because there are just too many products on the marketplace. This means that readers will often only skim-read your listings to make a decision about whether or not they want to purchase your product. The bullet points found at the top of your listing are typically the only things customers will read about your product.

Understanding that this is all a customer will read is important when writing your product listing. You would need to strategically place information on your listing to highlight all the features that your customers might be looking for. Below are a few helpful highlights you can use to increase your product information in your bullet points:

- **Add the best features first:** Ensure that your first bullet point is captivating; otherwise, readers may lose interest in your product. Your product's best feature should always be in the first bullet point.

- **Write in caps:** To draw customers' attention to the most important features of your products, you can write them in caps. This is because you will be restricted from using tools like bolding when writing your bullet points.

- **Keep it short and sweet:** Don't add too much unnecessary information to your bullet points because you risk losing the attention of your customers. Your bullet points should preferably be only one sentence containing only the most important information.

Bullet points are what draw your customers' eyes, so taking advantage of them will definitely work in your favor - if done correctly.

Visuals That Are Engaging

Our brains have the ability to process images up to 60,000 times faster than words. Keeping this in mind when setting up your product listing will ultimately lead to the success of your product. Use enticing images to improve the attractiveness of your listing and increase the chances of having your products sold. You can use the following tips to capture the attention of your customers:

- **High-resolution images:** It is recommended by Amazon that all images used are at least 1,000 pixels in either height or width.

- **Multiple photos:** Using multiple photos when creating your listing will help customers build trust in your brand and have confidence when choosing your product.

- **Edit your photos:** To increase the attention of your buyers, you should edit your photos by increasing your exposure, reducing shadows, and fixing the contrast to allow the colors of your images to stand out.

It will pay off if you take the time to source and edit your photos, and you will be able to grab the attention of your readers and build their trust.

Drive Sales With a Carefully Crafted Listing

Your product listing is the place where your product has the opportunity to shine. This will also convince readers to care about and ultimately buy your products. If you are selling a unique item, you have the opportunity to choose the right images and information to add to your listings to motivate customers to make a purchase. You should take your time and use all the tips I provided you with to ensure that you create the perfect listing for your products.

Tips to Optimize Amazon Product Listings

To drive traffic to your Amazon store, you should optimize your listings on Amazon. This can be done easily while providing customers with the branded store experience they may be looking for. The following tips will help you optimize your listings and implement new opportunities.

Amazon Brand Registry Application

Amazon's Brand Registry is an offering by Amazon that is not used by many e-commerce companies, although it can help validate your company and you can register multiple brands under one name. You can gain detailed page control using this function, as well as report intellectual property and counterfeit infringements. You will be provided with various tools that will help you not only build but also protect your brand and help your customers easily navigate through your store.

Track Amazon Listings

Managing your inventory is an essential part of being an Amazon seller. You should create a spreadsheet and keep track of all your listings. You should take note of your ASIN, or Amazon Standard Identification Number, as well as the 10-digit alphanumeric number that Amazon provides you with. A single ASIN number is used by Amazon to tie up all UPC numbers, so you would need to establish if any of your primary barcodes are already in use. This can be done manually by going to the inventory tab, clicking on *Add a Product*, and entering the UPC code.

Keep Track of Amazon Listings

Your next step would be to inventory the sellers who have made those listings. You can do this by choosing to view all the available listings those sellers have; this can be done by clicking on the seller's name and you will be redirected to their storefront. You should then create a new tab on your spreadsheet and add the seller's display name and seller ID. You can then add any and all ASIN codes they have on their profile.

I recommend adding their ID when entering their information into the spreadsheet, as sellers have the ability to change their names at any time, which will make it more difficult for you to find them again. Their ID remains the same no matter how many times they choose to change their names.

Manage Your Amazon Listing Regularly

You can upload your listings once you have optimized them. You would want to use the UPC code assigned to your product as your product ID. This will allow Amazon to see if there are current listings with the same code and whether it is already assigned to an ASIN. You should save a copy of your template and add your ASIN code as a reference. You also need to paste the ASIN code over the UPC code in the product ID.

Your next step is to change the update delete field to Partial Update. This process should be repeated as many times as you receive in your upload report, and you should upload your template again. The values in the back end of Amazon will be overridden as well as the Brand Registry, which will push updates to the detail page. This will be completed anywhere within fifteen minutes to twenty-four hours.

You would need to do a Partial Update using your product ID when selling a registered brand, and you should ensure that you add all the necessary information in the first section of your template. You will then receive a GCID for your products once the Brand Registry has been mobilized.

You can check which one of your brands is currently activated by going to *Brand Registry* and clicking on *reports*, then *Business reports*, and finally *Brand Performance*. You will find a list of all your products that have been activated under the Brand Registry here.

Communicating with Other Sellers is Not Allowed

Seller-to-seller communication within Amazon has been stopped since a new policy was released in 2018. Amazon's terms of service clearly state the following:

'This form is for use by Amazon customers to ask product-related questions of sellers on our third-party platforms (Amazon Marketplace and Merchants). The use of this form to send unrelated messages to sellers is strictly prohibited."

Report Copyright, Trademark, Counterfeit, and Listing Abuse Infringement

The policy that is being violated should be clearly stated when you contact Amazon concerning fellow sellers. You should also add that infringements are against the listing itself when it comes to duplicate listings or trademarks being found in the competitor's title. This will help you to remove any unauthorized IP use without creating a large number of emails from merchants who might have been selling on that listing without being aware of the infringement.

You would need to acknowledge the following statement when submitting an infringement report. This statement is so you understand the infringement that you will be reporting and what the consequences might be when submitting your complaint against other sellers should they be false or inaccurate:

"As an Amazon seller, I understand that submitting false or inaccurate complaints against other sellers may result in the suspension or termination of my Amazon selling privileges."

Duplicate Listings: Listings that are the same are considered to be duplicates, with one key difference, the duplicate listing is listed under the reseller's UPC. The goal of this policy is to remove any duplicate listings that may become inactive.

Trademark infringement: When another seller uses your trademarked brand name in their title, copy, or display name, they may be liable for trademark infringement. The goal of this Amazon policy is to remove any trademarked terms from a listing by the seller performance team.

Counterfeit products: Counterfeit products are often lower-quality products used to deceive customers. The goal of this Amazon policy is to eliminate any listings by sellers that might contain counterfeit products.

Copyright infringement: Copyright infringement occurs when another seller uses your images or directly copies your information to use on their listing. The goal of this policy is to remove any copyrighted information from other listings.

Detail page listing abuse: This policy describes when a seller has an offer that doesn't match the detail page description. The aim is to remove any infringing sellers from offering listings on your product detail page or bundle.

Merging Duplicate ASINs

You can merge duplicate ASINs; this is to keep Amazon's platform clean. Amazon sales will be hurt if products are listed more than once and customers get confused. Brand owners will also receive a variety of benefits, like an increased number of reviews on their products and being able to track resellers for a specific listing.

Remember that everything on Amazon can be undone, including the unmerging of ASINs. If you find that merging ASINs causes issues you can request to have them unmerged when needed. Amazon may opt to unmerge ASINs at any time should they find that complications arise.

Change Listings VIA the Category Department

Should you find that there are any issues with your detail page updates, you would need to file them with the Catalog Department. This department is responsible for maintaining the growing Amazon catalog. They are also able to assist with merging and unmerging ASINs, removing child ASINs from parents, and removing other sellers 'contributions to the Brand Registry.

Enforce Distribution

Before a product shows up on Amazon, it has to go through distribution enforcement through a brand's supply chain. The official stance of Amazon on Distribution Enforcement is as follows:

"Amazon respects a manufacturer's right to enter into exclusive distribution agreements for its products. However, violations of such agreements do not constitute intellectual property rights infringement. As the enforcement of these agreements is a matter between the manufacturer and the retailers, it would not be appropriate for Amazon to assist in enforcement activities."

To have a clear brand presence on Amazon, it is essential to have individual reseller agreements with your distributors. It is also important to accurately control your inventory so you can see by whom and where your products are being sold.

Fact Box:
Throughout this chapter, I covered the following:

- What an Amazon product listing is and how it works.

- What you need to add to your product listing.

- How to create the perfect product listing.

- How you can drive sales with the right product listing.

- Helpful tips to help you optimize your product listing.

Segue: In the next chapter, I will teach you how to direct traffic toward your Amazon shop.

Chapter 6:

Pulling Traffic towards your shop

Key Takeaway: Your products and listings may be great - but you won't sell anything without getting the right people to your shop.

"Quickly understand where a website's traffic comes from and what devices visitors prefer to use. On Amazon.com, desktops drive 39.4% of visits, while 60.6% of visitors come from mobile devices" (Semrush, n.d.).

What is Traffic and How Should You Interpret It?

Web Traffic is Important - But Not the Only Thing

When e-commerce was first introduced, there weren't a lot of ways that could be used to establish how a website was performing. Analyzing website performance became more comprehensive as digital marketers got smarter. Website analysts are no longer just asking how many visitors a website received; instead, they are checking on all of the following:

How long visitors were on the site: It doesn't matter how many visitors a site receives if these visitors only look at the website for a few seconds. You are able to see the behavior of users by looking at the bounce rate and time-on-page statistics of your website.

Percentage of users making purchases: Your website conversion rate will show you how many of your users are actually making purchases. It is important to check this because it doesn't matter if you have a large audience if you are not making the necessary sales. The conversion rate will also show you whether you are effectively marketing your products.

Costs related to drawing in traffic: Various e-commerce businesses rely on paid traffic to bring new customers to their stores. This type of paid traffic can be in the form of PPC (pay-per-click) ads or affiliates. The two most important metrics have to be CAC (Cost of Acquiring Customers) and CPA (Cost Per Acquisition). You are able to adjust the amount you are spending on ads by balancing them with your AOV (Average Order Value) and your CLV (Customer Lifetime Value).

How is Website Traffic Actually Recorded?

A website's server is connected to your computer or other devices that can connect to the web. There are dozens of distinct files that make up each web page. Every file gets transmitted by the site server to the user's browser, where they are formed into one cumulative hit containing text and graphics. Each file that is sent is represented as a "hit" and you can receive multiple hits through one view on your site.

The various sections of your website are constantly monitored by the server to see how many hits it receives. Each site visit is called a "session." There is a beginning and an endpoint for every session, and the time of a site visit often varies. Every request on your site is recorded by the server; this data allows you to see how popular your site is and how many times your link is clicked. You are also able to see which sections of your site get the most attention from visitors. The "server log" is used to record every request that the website receives. Entries from across posterity are captured on the log, and this creates a database that the website owner can then use to understand the activity their website receives.

The Importance of External Traffic for Your Amazon Business

Why is External Traffic Important?

One of the most important ways in which you can build your position on Amazon is by generating as much traffic as possible. This will also help you increase your profits. The presence of your brand will also grow if you monitor your external traffic closely. You will be able to achieve the following with external traffic:

Gain Amazon Rewards: Amazon prides itself in rewarding sellers who are able to generate external traffic to their listings. This is because Amazon wants as much traffic as it can get to its site, and it's just that much better if these visits are translated into sales.

Drive Traffic: The main reason that anyone would invest in Amazon Ads is to make sales. Although you will be able to reach your goals faster if you combine these ads with external traffic. Your brand profile, recall, and visibility will increase when you start using external ads.

When you struggle with your ranking using only the tools provided by Amazon, then you should definitely consider using external ads. You will have control over where your sales are coming from while you work on improving your platform performance.

Boost Brand Awareness: Another bonus of driving external traffic is that your brand will stand out from your competitors. It may be difficult to obtain Amazon visibility, just like getting to the top of Google searches. Another obstacle you might face is differentiating your brand because of the strict regulations and formats that Amazon has set. To ensure that quality is consistent, there is a certain uniformity when selling on Amazon. This does however limit your creative thinking because it is often looked on unfavorably.

When advertising off-Amazon, you can think more creatively, and you are able to showcase the positive aspects of your products.

Improve Keyword Ranking: Your sales numbers will increase significantly as you start generating more sales. Increasing your traffic is a great way of improving your Best Seller Rank. Traffic from other sites is simply supplementing Amazon's organic traffic and the marketing activities that Amazon offers. Advertising off-Amazon is a better option than just relying on Amazon alone or hoping that buyers will come across your listing themselves.

Beat the Competition: The possibility of competition is always there, especially if you are selling a product that people are truly interested in. It's always a positive thing to have some healthy competition because it allows you to think of ways to outperform your competitors. You should always look for other platforms that you can use to get your products in front of potential customers.

Find New Audiences: Keep in mind that when a customer purchases your product through the platform itself, then that customer belongs to Amazon. You are able to control this by implementing a few things. When advertising off-Amazon you will ultimately be the first point of contact for customers, and from there you can point them to your listings. Building a powerful brand is easier if you have an effective business model in place, allowing you to sell your products more effectively. You should start generating sales yourself if you truly want to reach success.

How to Drive Traffic to Your Amazon Store

Learning how to drive traffic is possibly one of the most important skills for starting an ecommerce business with Amazon. In the following section, I will provide you with three proven ways to drive traffic to your Amazon store.

Improve Your Organic Ranking

Consumers will often start their product searches on Amazon instead of using Google for their search. Increasing your organic ranking will help your products come up in search results, which helps you get discovered. You want your products to show up on the first page of Amazon searches. This is because customers rarely move to the second or third pages of Amazon to look for products. The most effective way of improving your organic ranking is to perform proper keyword research and targeting is. Attempt to stay away from high-competition keywords that may be difficult to rank for. You should look for low-hanging keywords that don't have much competition but can still provide you with good traffic. If you use a mix of these keywords, you will show up more in organic search results.

Optimize Your Listing

The following factors are all taken into consideration when your keyword ranking is determined:

- number of products sold

- the velocity of sales

- feedback from you as the seller

- positive reviews

Your product listing optimization heavily affects your rankings. This means that you would need to optimize your listings in order to increase your search result visibility. You can use the following to achieve this:

- Add primary keywords to your title.

- Add your brand name to your title.

- When writing your content, add primary keywords.

- In order to make your content easier to read, put them in bullet points.

- Place important keywords throughout your product description.

- Images that are high-quality and informative should be added to your listings.

- Properly categorize your products.

- Instead of creating different listings, add various colors and sizes to your initial listings.

Amazon sellers need to create optimized product listings to ensure they rank high on Amazon and Google search engines.

Run Effective PPC Campaigns

We all know that it takes time to build up organic traffic for your business. This is why you should make use of PPC or Pay-Per-Click ads. You will be able to show your products to potential customers, whether they search for your specific keywords or not. You should, however, ensure that your keyword bid is still competitive enough.

You will be able to get a lot of traffic when running effective PPC campaigns for your Amazon business. Even when launching a new product, you can generate significant traffic. Your advertising cost is the only thing you would need to worry about when running PPC campaigns. To avoid too much bidding, I recommend that you use low-competition keywords that still provide good traffic.

Fact Box:
Throughout this chapter, I covered the following:

- What exactly is traffic, and how you should use it.

- Web traffic is not everything.

- How traffic is recorded on your Amazon store.

- Why you should drive external traffic to your store.

- How you can drive traffic to your store.

- How to run effective PPC campaigns.

Segue: You will be learning about the importance of great customer reviews throughout the following chapter.

Chapter 7:

Getting great reviews

Key Takeaway: Good ratings and reviews give your shop integrity and social proof, so be sure to take good care of your customers and motivate them to speak about their positive shopping experience.

"In research conducted by Dixa this year, 93% of customers will read online reviews before making a purchase, with 47% spreading the word about a positive experience and a striking 95% shouting from the rooftops about a negative experience." (Loiselle, 2021)

Based on the above statistics, you can see that customer reviews play a big role in your success on Amazon FBA. Consumers depend on reviews to make informed decisions on the purchases they make. They also depend on reviews to see what other customers experienced and what problems they had with their orders. Reviews also tell potential customers how their complaints have been addressed and whether or not products live up to the claims that you as the seller are making.

Customers are less likely to purchase a product if there are no customer reviews; this is why it's important to ensure your products get as many positive reviews as possible.

Why Are Reviews Important?

Reviews are important when you are looking to turn your Amazon listing into an e-commerce powerhouse. I will be providing you with some valuable tips to get more positive reviews for your listings so you can increase your sales, optimize your conversion rate, and improve your ranking on Amazon.

You should however be aware of the gray areas related to the review, like paying for reviews that can lead to costly sanctions and being banished from Amazon. Doing this will not be worth the risk of losing your Amazon store. I want to teach you how to get reviews not only quickly, but legally.

Why Are Reviews Important on Amazon?

"89% of global consumers read reviews as part of their buying journey, while 49% consider positive reviews one of the top three buying influences."

Ratings and reviews are important to you as an Amazon store owner because they will allow you to reap the rewards, but you might be asking why this is.

The short answer is trust. Consumers are more likely to trust the opinion of others than take a listing at face value. This means that buyers will often look at what other people have to say about a brand or product before making a purchase themselves. Amazon reviews are often compared with each other when having to choose between two similar products.

If your product has, for example, a 4.3 out of 5 score based on reviews by 1,000 customers, you are more likely to make sales than when you have a 4.5 out of 5 score based on only 11 reviews. The more reviews you have, the more social proof is provided to potential buyers about the quality of your product and the level of service you are providing to your customers. This will increase your trustworthiness even more than a higher ranking ever will.

Another benefit that reviews have is that they provide you with feedback that you can then use to improve your product. They allow you to get a better understanding of what your customers like or do not like about your product.

You should also be aware of the rules clearly laid out by Amazon regarding reviews, and I will explain these rules below:

Amazon Rules on Reviews

The rules that Amazon has set up regarding reviews are to ensure that customers are protected and that the authenticity of the reviews is protected. These rules should not be taken lightly, as there are sanctions set out by Amazon for these types of violations.

In a nutshell, any reviews that are unnatural or inorganic are viewed as violations. This means that you are not able to do the following:

- Get paid reviews.

- Create accounts and leave fake reviews on your own products.

- Get negative reviews removed by customers.

- Ask family or friends to leave reviews on your products.

- Give your own product a review.

- Divert negative reviews.

Sophisticated algorithms are used by Amazon to pick up on these illegitimate methods, and they will punish you as the seller for using them.

This is why I recommend that you only use validated methods of gaining reviews; otherwise, you might risk losing the trust of your customers and ruining your hard work. You should always build social proof by getting valid reviews from real customers if you are looking to increase your sales and gain new customers.

Why You Should Never Buy Amazon Reviews

How We Spot A Phoney Review

As time has gone by, we as customers have started looking at reviews more critically to ensure that we are getting what we are paying for. There are various companies turning to paid reviews in order to increase their star ratings and make more sales.

If you have ever seen a new product from a company that doesn't have a website with over 15,000 five-star reviews within a very short period, then you can be sure that these are compensated reviews. These reviews, however, violate the terms of service that Amazon has set up, and they are often hard to keep track of.

Compensated reviews work in the following way: Businesses pay individuals to create accounts on Amazon and then purchase their products and leave a four or five-star review. Doing so makes it difficult for Amazon to keep track of these reviews because they are indeed based on purchases. There are pay-for-review sites that even ask their reviewers to leave negative comments on various products sold by businesses that are not clients in order to make the reviews seem more authentic and not like they are compensated.

The Vine Program

In essence, the Vine program involves giving away free products or providing products at a significant discount to potential customers in exchange for their honest reviews on Amazon. These reviews can also be somewhat problematic.

Examples of some of the problems that may occur include not following up on breakage concerns or customer service, and reviewers might not take the purchase and shipping processes into consideration because they are getting the product for free.

Another consideration to keep in mind is that the opinion of reviewers might be affected because they are getting products either entirely or partially free. These reviewers are often negative or more critical than buyers who may not be asked to leave a review. A product might seem a little less irritating if it is not paid for by an individual.

Also keep in mind that reviewers might not be able to give informed reviews because they are uneducated about the product and have no real experience with it; therefore, they may also have no reference about how something else would work in comparison. It may be difficult to leave an honest review because these reviewers are unaware of what other products are available to them.

How to Get Great, Authentic Reviews For Your Products

I will provide you with five tips for getting authentic reviews for your products in the following section:

Provide Great Customer Experience

Product misinformation is possibly the number one reason why customers leave negative reviews. You should always be honest about the products you are selling and be as accurate as possible when providing information to avoid confusion and false expectations.

Send Follow-Up Emails Asking for Feedback

Amazon sends emails to your customers after a purchase is made, but keep in mind that these emails are generic and have nothing special about them. I recommend that you send personalized review requests when a customer makes a purchase of one of your products, this should be done as soon as a product is delivered to a customer so their experience of your product is still fresh in their minds.

Request Reviews VIA Newsletters and Social Media

The fans you have on Facebook and the people who are subscribed to your newsletter probably already like you, so why don't you ask them to give you reviews on your products? If they have already received a product from you, then the chances are they can provide you with legitimate and positive feedback about their experience.

Reach Out to Users Who Reviewed Similar Products

Another way of getting reviews is by looking up other products similar to yours and taking a look at who reviewed those products. You can then get in contact with these individuals and ask them to leave reviews for your own products. You should take note of these competitors and read the reviews they receive on their products.

Solicit the Top Amazon Reviewers

One key thing to remember is that Amazon often keeps a list of its top reviewers. These are reviewers who are valued for their opinions and objective reviews. Some of these reviewers have titles like "Top Ten Reviewer" or "Hall of Fame Reviewer." These titles are often shown next to their reviews, which makes their reviews more valuable.

Fact Box:
Throughout this chapter, I covered the following:

- Why product reviews are important.
- Review rules from Amazon.
- Why buying Amazon reviews can be dangerous.
- What to look out for to spot false reviews.
- How to get the best product reviews.
- How to provide your customers with a great experience.
- How to reach out to customers to get reviews.

Segue: As we are approaching the final chapter, I will be showing you how you can grow your

Amazon business further, once you manage to establish yourself.

Chapter 8:

Growing your Business

Further

Key Takeaway: A healthy business should always look for ways to grow and get better.

"There is still room for Amazon to continue growing in the long run, notwithstanding its size in absolute terms and market leadership in the eCommerce space. AMAZON's revenue is expected to grow by a CAGR of +12.6% for the FY 2023–2026 period according to S&P Capital IQ." (Amazon.com. Inc, 2022)

Amazon FBA Trends you Should Be Aware Of

Consumers Will Purchase More Products From Social Media Platforms

Social media has evolved significantly over the past few years, giving customers the opportunity to purchase products through posts, videos, and ads. More and more social media giants are aiming to challenge the dominance that Amazon has in the e-commerce world.

"The term 'social commerce 'seems to be getting more popular each year as younger generations trust people's opinions on what to buy more than they do big brands." (Jake Zaratsian).

"Social media will become an even bigger driver of e-commerce in 2023. The giants like TikTok and Meta will continue adapting their offerings, but I suspect we'll also see new social media platforms emerge that will also try to tap into the e-commerce space." (Lenny Smith).

Amazon expert, seller, and influencer—these will all become job titles in the future.

"With influencer marketing picking up, I think the Amazon Attribution feature and video campaigns will take off on Amazon. I think Amazon will find new placements that open up more opportunities for sellers to win bids and expand their sponsored brand video campaign spend." (Jake Zaratsian).

Virtual Reality Will Play A Bigger Role in eCommerce

Virtual reality will break into the e-commerce world in a big way in 2023. Virtual reality will change the customer experience in a big way and will give e-commerce a huge advantage.

Advertising Off Amazon Will Be More Important Than Ever For Amazon Sellers

It has never been more important than now to create diverse and far-reaching ads for your Amazon listings. This will also help you stay far ahead of your competitors.

"I think 2023 will bring more advertising platforms for e-commerce sellers, and I think we'll also see more maturity in the existing platforms, offering more features to help sellers" (Lenny Smith).

It may become more difficult to stand out from the competition as you start improving your advertising. One way that you can advertise to stand out above the competition is to take your advertising off-platform.

"One of the biggest advertising trends is going to be marketing off Amazon and pointing things to your specific listing on Amazon" (Mike Scheschuk).

"Customers Ask Alexa" Will Become an Invaluable Tool For Sellers

The feature "Customers ask Alexa" was launched by Amazon in 2022 to give selected brands the opportunity to give answers to questions posed to Alexa by customers. They are also able to provide links and references to products that will solve the problem these customers might have. This feature will be made available to all registered brands in 2023 which will definitely change Amazon's e-commerce experience.

Sourcing Will Continue To Move Closer to North America

Experienced sellers are changing their mindsets related to shipping and stocking.

"I think (and hope) we are getting closer to more sellers seeing the benefit of sourcing closer to the United States. If we experience another Covid-like shutdown in China, I believe this could be the tipping point that pushes brands to think outside of the box in order to avoid manufacturing their products there" (Jake Zaratsian).

Strategies to Grow Your Amazon FBA Business

Amazon's A to Z Will go A-er to Z-er

Amazon aims to make every customer's experience excellent with its A to Z promise. To improve this, you as an Amazon seller would need to ensure that your products are always of high quality. Paying attention to small details will allow you to help grow your Amazon business.

Tap Into the International Market

There are essentially two proven ways in which you can reach international markets with your Amazon business:

- Sign up with the 10 marketplaces and advertise your products.

- Make use of Amazon Global Selling so they can ship your products to buyers all over the world.

Expand Your Paid Advertising Possibilities

Amazon's sponsored products are a great tool to use, no matter what your advertising budget is. You will only pay when your ads are clicked, and you can decide how much money you are willing to pay. This is a very low-risk, high-return model to use when you are looking to grow your business.

Offer Amazon Prime To Your Customers

There has been a huge increase in Amazon Prime users over the past few years, so why wouldn't you take advantage of it? There are also various benefits that come with Amazon Prime, including tapping into the 185 countries that Amazon delivers to. You will also have access to over one billion items that are sold by Amazon.

Never Let Negative Review Slip Past You

Thinking that one or two negative reviews won't affect your business can be extremely dangerous. These negative reviews can ultimately affect how customers see your business, especially when they are left unattended. To become successful with Amazon FBA, you should take every small negative review as an opportunity to improve not only your products but your service as well. Doing this will help you stay ahead of your competitors while increasing your profits.

Hold Yourself to Account

Holding yourself accountable is another important aspect that you need to improve on to become and stay successful with Amazon. You should start taking accountability by making a list of between three and five minor and major things that you can improve on.

Take Prime Now For A Test Drive

Prime Now is an offering that Amazon has made available to merchants who already have an active Amazon FBA business. It gives buyers the opportunity to receive their products within one to four hours. How your business is currently doing will be the deciding factor in whether or not you qualify for Amazon Prime Now. If you do not qualify, I recommend that you work on the weak points of your business and start selling fancier things. You should also start delegating tasks better if you find that you are struggling to keep up with orders.

10 Expert Ways of Growing Your FBA Business

Optimize Your Inventory

- Ensure that your prices are always competitive.

- Correct any product listing you are not happy with.

- Make use of Amazon Sponsored Ads

- Use eBay to sell any inventory you currently have in Amazon warehouses.

Clean Your Back-End Metrics

- Perform a health checkup.

- Look for any negative or neutral feedback and remove them.

- Take a look at any dead inventory you might have and get rid of it.

- Take stock of any returned inventory.

Improve Yourself

- Keep learning

- Clean your office space to give yourself mental clarity.

An Inspiring Story: How Entrepreneurs Build Seven-Figure Amazon FBA Businesses

How to Start a Seven-Figure Amazon FBA Business in 2023

Choose a Niche

The product you choose to sell should not just be something you saw and thought would generate sales. You should take your time to look for a product that you not only have knowledge of and experience with but that is also selling well on Amazon. This first step is not easy but may be the most important to ensure success.

Jeff Bezos stated the following on the topic:

"I very frequently get the question: 'What's going to change in the next 10 years? 'And that is a very interesting question, it is a very common one. I almost never get the question: 'What is not going to change in the next 10 years? 'And I submit to you that the second question is actually the more important of the two because you can build a business strategy around the things that are stable in time. When you have something that you know is true, even over the long term, you can afford to put a lot of energy into it."

Some of the most important questions that you should be asking yourself when picking your niche include:

- What am I passionate about and interested in building a brand around?

- Is there a specific type of person that you would like to help with the sale of your product?

- Are there buyers for your specific product?

- Will the product still be popular in 10 years and is the market growing?

- Will I be willing to invest my time and attention in this product for the next two to five years?

- Will I be willing to build an online marketing strategy both on and off Amazon with this product?

Keep in mind that this business is not a get-rich-quick thing and takes time and attention to build.

Find a Product

In this step, you can use the Amazon bestseller list to help you make an informed decision about the product you choose. Some of the key things that you should keep in mind are:

- Pricing is between $15 and $50 to ensure that you make a profit.

- The product should weigh less than 2 lbs so you don't pay too much for shipping.

- The seller rank should be under 1500 because this shows high demand.

There are a few ways in which you can start selling on Amazon. These include:

- Create and manufacture your own products.

- Buy cheap items at garage sales and sell them for a profit on Amazon.

- Find and improve products that are already making sales on Amazon.

- Find and sell popular products under your own brand.

There is a lot of opportunity available with Amazon since they are already selling over 12 million different products to their U.S. audience alone. You should aim to find products that are in high demand that you can market better than the competition and turn a profit on.

The demand for a Product: By looking at the Best Seller Rank of a product, you will be able to see if there is a demand for that product. You can find the ranking of a product by scrolling down to the "Product Information" section of a listing. The Best Seller Rank is updated hourly and shows you exactly how many sales the product has made.

Keep in mind that if a product has a low BSR, then it is making a lot of sales, whereas if the BSR is higher, then the product might not be performing well. This is, however, just an indication because some categories might be more popular than others. For example, products under the Home and Kitchen category can be seen as best sellers with a BSR of below 1500, whereas products under the Arts and Crafts category would need a BSR of below 500 to be classified as products that are making sales.

This means that you would need to look at the actual monthly sales of a product to make an informed decision.

You should also take the following into consideration:

- products selling throughout the year and not just seasonally

- the improvement potential of a product

- and manufacturing simplicity

Competition Assessment: Once you have determined which products are the most popular, it is time to take a look at the competition that you will be facing. This step shouldn't take too much time because if you market the product that you choose effectively, you will without a doubt outperform most Amazon sellers. You should preferably choose a product with fewer than 500 reviews, but this should not be a deciding factor. You should be willing to work on building your brand instead of competing with reviews, pricing, and keywords.

Sourcing Your Product

Alibaba, GlobalSource, and DHGate are great examples of suppliers you are able to use to source your products. These suppliers are also your best option because they are already affiliated with Amazon and know what should be done regarding all sections. You will also save yourself a lot of time on research when using these suppliers.

Start looking for companies that manufacture products that you can sell under your own private label. You can do this by going to the sites mentioned above and typing in the keywords for your chosen product. You will then be given the various supplies that you can use to purchase the product you want to sell.

It might be a little intimidating to find the right supplier for your business, especially because you are tying up funds in purchasing inventory, and you don't want a supplier who might run away with your money. You should always perform due diligence so you can be sure a supplier is who they are claiming to be and is not just another scam artist. Once you have your product and supplier picked out, you should start negotiating.

Negotiation Tips: When entering into negotiations with your suppliers, you should imagine that you are at a garage sale, car boot sale, Sunday market, or fair with various stalls selling the same product. You should imagine going to the first stall and asking them for their best price, then telling them that you would get back to them before moving to the next stall. You should do this at every stall, comparing the products and prices as you go. This will help you determine who is offering the best prices without compromising on the quality of the product being offered.

You should do this with at least four to five stalls, telling each one that you are looking to buy the products in bulk but that you first want to test the market to see if the product will sell.

You can then ask to take a test order, and should the product sell, you will place an order of a thousand, and perhaps tens of thousands, depending on the sales you will be making. A few other aspects that you would need to consider when choosing your supplier are the ease of communication, response speed, product quality, quotes on branding, quotes for shipping, and what your gut is telling you. You need to go in with your eyes wide open when attempting to negotiate. Below are some useful tips you can use when going into negotiations.

- Thoroughly research every feature of your chosen product. You can achieve this by looking at all the product reviews, both positive and negative as this will give you a clear indication of any improvements that you need to make. It will also help when you are going to suppliers to discuss the product.

- Start a conversation with your supplier instead of starting off with the price and quantity you need. Inform your supplier that you have an ecommerce business and you are looking to expand your business through working with great suppliers.

- Be calm and courteous. You should always keep cultural differences in mind when attempting to source products from other countries. When talking with potential suppliers, always do so with respect and try to understand that they may not always understand what you are requesting the first time. This means that you would need to be as clear and descriptive as possible, especially when there is a language barrier.

- One rule to remember is that everything is negotiable. Never settle on the first price you are offered. You can use email, skype, and phone to enter into negotiations with your suppliers.

- You should be willing to pay 30% of the purchase amount on order and the other 70% before your products are shipped. Always ensure that you get pictures of your products before they leave your supplier's warehouse and always pay via credit card or PayPal so you can claim your funds back should your stock not arrive.

- If you follow all the steps provided above it's time to relax and believe that everything will go smoothly from here. Remember that when you build a relationship with your suppliers, then they are less likely to let you down and have your stock go missing.

Testing your products: After completing the steps laid out above, you should request a sample of the product from each of your suppliers. This should be done before you place an order for larger quantities. Your product quality is extremely important because if you sell a bad product, then your customers will have no problem telling everyone about their experience. Remember that your customers will be far happier leaving a negative review than a positive review. It is still your job to seek out good suppliers and stay away from the bad ones.

Building relationships: This is something well worth mentioning because it is key if you are attempting to grow your business. You should build relationships with your suppliers so you know you are doing business with people you like and trust. You can also visit your suppliers so you can see firsthand how your products are made and negotiate with them face-to-face. You will also feel more comfortable with the products you are selling if you know exactly how they are made. Establishing a relationship with your suppliers may lead to better rates and credit terms over time.

Establishing your brand: When creating your marketing strategy, it's important to keep your brand in mind. There is no doubt about how tough it is to create a brand for your product. You can ask yourself the following questions when thinking about how to brand your products.

- What are your values and what do you stand for?

- Will your customers 'lives improve with your brand?

- When customers come across your brand, what are the five emotions you would want them to feel?

- When using your products or services, what is a deeper reason customers might have?

- Are you able to translate that into your brand message?

- What do the brand and private label products of your competitors look like?

- Will you be able to improve?

- How are other brands communicating with their customers?

Your brand name: When creating a seller account with Amazon, you will essentially have two names:

1. **Your Seller Name:** This is the name that you use when registering your business, and the name your listing will be under. If you are looking at only having one niche, then this name can be the same as your brand name. But if you are looking to add other niche products to

your business then you might want to create a company name that is not niche specific. (This has been covered in a previous chapter).

2. **Your Product Brand Name:** With every product that you sell on Amazon you can create a unique brand name, especially when selling products in different categories. These different brand names will however still fall under your main company name.

"Your seller display name is displayed with your listing and on your Seller Profile. Sellers are generally allowed to be as descriptive or fanciful as they like when creating their display names. There are a few constraints, however."

- A unique display name should be provided by every seller.

- The word "Amazon" may not be included in your display name.

- The rights to your display name should be entirely your own.

- No special characters except "-" and "_" may be used in your display name.

- Offensive and profane words are not allowed.

- Display names with less than 20 characters are recommended.

You should take your time to come up with the perfect display name. Remember that your brand name and design can be changed at any time and is not permanent. Your focus should be to get started, so don't let something like your brand name hold you up.

Create Your Brand and Design

Your brand and design will undoubtedly either help grow your business or be the reason for its failure. Take your time to create an intriguing and interesting brand for your products, and you will see profits in no time. Your brand will ultimately include your name and logo.

You have two options when creating a design for your brand:

- Brand the product itself by printing on it or creating stickers.

- Leave the product as is and brand the packaging you will be using.

Essentially, it doesn't matter which option you choose because you will still need to pay for the manufacturing of your branding material. This means you would need to find out what the costs are for branding. You would then have to get your brand designed. This can be created yourself or you can hire someone to do it for you. You should ask your manufacturer for the specifications of your product or packaging so you can base your design on this information.

Getting your design right doesn't have to happen with your first product, instead, aim to get your first product listed and then improve on your brand design as your business grows and you start making profits.

Create Your Seller Account

You might think that you should just jump in and create your seller account with Amazon, but keep in mind that if you don't start making sales immediately, you would be paying a monthly fee without getting anything back. Before you set up your seller account, make sure you have your product images, listings, keywords, and launch strategy ready. This is so you can ensure that you will be able to start selling immediately after creating your seller account.

Shipping Your Product

This step might seem a little intimidating, but the reality is that if you choose the right suppliers, you won't need to do anything because they will handle the shipping on your behalf.

When shipping your products to Amazon warehouses, you can choose to do so by air or sea. I suggest that you discuss shipping options with your supplier, but you will likely be paying around $6 for every kilogram, and your shipping time would likely be between 8 and 10 working days.

If you are unhappy with the shipping quote that you receive from your supplier, then you might want to get in direct contact with an air express company. You can start shipping by sea once you start ordering quantities of 5,000 or more.

Using a third-party inspection service: A third-party inspection company will serve as the middleman between you or your manufacturer and the Amazon warehouse. They will inspect your products and store them until you are ready to have them shipped to an Amazon warehouse.

This is a great option for the following reasons:

- It's cheaper than storing your products at an Amazon warehouse and you can ship smaller amounts of your products as you need them.

- It's always a good idea to have your products inspected before they are shipped to buyers, especially when you are just starting your business and supplier relationships are not yet established. You need to make sure that the quality of your products is as high as possible. You should also perform due diligence when choosing the company you would want to work with so you can be sure your needs are met.

Keep in mind that you would need to create shipping labels inside of Amazon whether your products are shipped directly from the manufacturer or from a third-party storage company.

Launching Your Product

The next thing you would need to do after this step is to tell as many people as possible that your products are now available on Amazon. You can also make use of the PPC campaigns available on Amazon, which will help you generate even more sales. Another way you can create exposure is by getting in touch with influencers and asking them to review your products and recommend them to their followers. There are various ways in which you can generate sales, and finding one that works for you and our business should be your goal.

You might be wondering what you should do once your products reach the Amazon fulfillment center. And I have compiled five steps that you can follow to launch your products; these include:

1. Optimizing your listing

    Add keywords to both your heading and bullet points, and ensure that you have between five and seven attractive images and a captivating description for your listing. You are also able to add a video to your listing if you are a brand seller, or create an image gallery with an interesting product description under your main listing. By presenting all the features and benefits of your product, your listing will stand out above the competition if you use every feature Amazon provides you.

Keep in mind that if you don't use the right keywords, you will not be found by customers. This is why you should ensure that your product shows up first when buyers are searching. The easiest way to achieve this is by using as many unique keywords as possible.

2. Focus on getting reviews

This is important no matter where your business with Amazon currently is. However, you should work on getting as many positive reviews as possible within the first few weeks of your products being listed. This should be your focus night and day. Reviewers will help you boost sales, come up with keywords, and increase the credibility of your product.

Although sellers are not allowed to solicit reviews anymore, you are still able to ask buyers for honest reviews regarding your products and service.

What would you want customers to see when they open your Amazon package? Is your product well presented, and have you included a note or instruction manual for it? Does your product do what you promised, and is it high quality? Will customers receive value for their money? These are all questions that should be considered when you expect to receive great reviews.

3. Invest in Amazon Sponsored Ads

You can start investing small amounts into Amazon Sponsored Ads, you can also choose the automatic option with Amazon PPC ads. Amazon will do all the work for you when you set a daily limit for your ads. You might not be able to spend $25 on ads every day when starting, but keep in mind that it will increase your listing's visibility. When using these ads, you will get valuable tips on which keywords you should be using as Amazon will tell you under which keywords your products are being found. You can then use this data on your manual campaigns to improve your products 'reach and visibility.

Create FAQs on your listing with keywords: Take a look at questions that were asked on your competitor's listings and use this data to add these questions and valuable answers to your listings to give buyers as much information as possible about your products. This will help you add value to your listing.

Use influencer marketing: Influencer marketing has seen a significant increase over the past few years, and tapping into it can help your business significantly. Start by finding bloggers and YouTubers who have large followings and ask them to review your products and suggest them to their followers. Ensure that they include your direct product link and offer a discount or special offer for their followers as a limited offer. During the first few days and weeks of your business, this can help with views, conversions, and sales. The "Amazon Stream" will kick in at this point, and you will start receiving organic sales from Amazon and the marketing they do for you.

You should do some sort of marketing every day if you want to outperform your competitors. Increasing your web presence, running ads, and finding reviewers is possibly the most important secret to achieving success.

Build Your Audience

Once again, one way of building an audience for your brand is by getting in contact with influencers in your niche who have a large following. This is one way of advertising your brand off-Amazon. This is important since there are millions of people in the world who have not bought from Amazon yet, and your product might just have them creating a buyer's account.

You can increase your ranking if you combine Amazon PPC ads with traffic that you generate from outside sources. One way of doing this is by building your email list, which will lead to long-term growth. You should work on building a network of people who are interested in buying your products and brand. These should be interested individuals that you can convert into buying customers.

Other off-Amazon methods: Building your audience off Amazon through social media, content marketing, and paid advertising through Google and Facebook.

Success Stories

Disclaimer: To protect the privacy of these entrepreneurs, their names have been changed.

Maria's Success Story

In 2015, this newly single mom of two was unemployed and had no idea how she was going to make a living and care for her children. Because of her pending divorce, she was left without a penny and highly stressed out financially.

Maria was worried about where she would live, how she would attend job interviews without a car, and how she would be able to afford an apartment. All of this caused her to live from day to day and only plan for the short term. This had become extremely exhausting, both emotionally, physically, and financially.

As she was researching ways to earn an income, she started looking into selling online but was scared because she didn't have the money or storage space. Since she was moving between family members 'houses, she wasn't able to purchase and store inventory. Maria came across Amazon FBA in her search. She wasn't aware that Amazon used third-party sellers and always assumed that products came directly from Amazon. After learning that she was able to send inventory to Amazon for them to store and ship her products, she felt that it was made for her.

As she started researching more, she saw that sellers were sourcing products from thrift stores, grocery markets, and even Walmart. She believed that if she put in the effort, she could also start a business like this, despite her limited resources.

Maria jumped into the business, starting with a very poor $300 credit limit. She jumped right in, and without spending tons of time researching, she visited kohls.com and found a kid's pirate ship being sold for $17.99 and decided to sell it on Amazon for $39.99. When she started, she expected to make $20 from the sale because she didn't have the Amazon Seller App to calculate and track the fees that she would need to pay to Amazon FBA for each sale. This was a huge mistake and not how she would have wanted to start her business. Needless to say, the pirate ships arrived on her doorstep two days later, and they were absolutely huge. This is when she knew she had done something wrong. Maria never checked the size of the product before ordering it, and it measured 12 feet in height and 14 feet in width.

She then decided to open an Amazon account and put in her first shipment. After a few days, 18 boxes of pirate ships were picked up by UPS, and she started doing what all Amazon sellers do—wait. The products arrived at the Amazon warehouse in California a week later, and she immediately noticed that the price had dropped, so she decided to drop hers too. Other sellers did the same; every time she dropped her price, others did the same. An hour later, she saw all of the pirate ships had been sold, but she had to pay Amazon $20 for each one that was sold. That led her to lose a few hundred dollars.

After the initial failure, Maria realized that her potential for profit was huge, especially after seeing how quickly her first products were sold. She saw the potential that Amazon had and decided to continue with her business idea. She realized that if she could find the right product, she could potentially make hundreds, if not thousands, of dollars daily.

She got to work by joining groups on Facebook, messaging other Amazon sellers, and watching as many YouTube videos as possible to gain the knowledge she needed. She jumped into the research that she should have done in the first place, and since she didn't have the money to attend an expensive course, she started looking for as much info as she could find online, and there was a lot. It just took a little searching and time.

At this stage, she had very little credit left in her attempt to turn her situation around. She went to a thrift store one day looking for a dress for her daughter and decided to see how much the board games they had available were selling on Amazon. She saw that these $2 games could actually be sold for $30–$40. This was not something that she would have preferred selling, and it took her a good while to go through every single board game box. Amazon requires these products to have every single piece before being listed. Some of the boxes were also shaped weirdly and were too big to fit into the standard shipping boxes. Despite the fact that these games took a lot of time to get ready for listing, they helped her build up capital. Maria then used those funds to move into the grocery, health and personal care, and business supply niches. Those board games helped her get her business going again.

After that, Maria moved into retail arbitrage and bought thousands of products that she then listed on her Amazon store. She used a connection she had at a local overstock warehouse to help her buy products in bulk. These products helped her gain 300% profit, which led to her building up capital very quickly. When she started her business, there weren't many resources regarding what was allowed, and sellers were getting suspended because they weren't following the rules. She then decided to create a business model that would last for years and could be sustained outside of Amazon. She started creating and launching her own products by contacting wholesale companies, assembling the products, and rebranding them under her own brand. She launched a total of 11 products, but only eight of them sold. Those eight products brought in a significant amount of money—more than she could have ever dreamt of.

This business owner is a living testament to how anyone can become successful with their Amazon business. Take the below stats for only one of her products, and if that doesn't show the income potential that Amazon has, I don't know what will. Keep in mind that just because she started earning an income, she didn't stop working on her business. She still works from home to provide her kids with the best life she can possibly provide them with.

Buy Box Percentage	100%
Units ordered	3,984
Unit session percentage	4,50%
Ordered product sales	$116,856.98

Total order items	3,840

Paul s Success Story

The next successful Amazon FBA business owner I would like to tell you about is a young U.S. Air Force officer. Paul started growing a passion for business while studying at the Air Force Academy, in part because he experienced the power of systems firsthand. When he left the military, after serving his country, he started building his business with Amazon FBA and started his digital marketing agency.

Since he joined the military at the tender age of 18, he was never able to experience the freedom that came from being an online entrepreneur. He had said that he wanted to solve his problems his way, and that turned into a highly profitable 7-figure Amazon FBA business. The organizational skills that he had learned from the military helped him become a successful entrepreneur, and he also found that he really enjoyed helping others. He used the systems that he had learned over the years to help him hire, train, and keep his digital marketing agency running smoothly.

He started his business with a forward-looking approach and always looked several steps ahead. He knew that Amazon was the way of the future and that the world would end up using it a lot.

He had built up his business and mastered the Amazon domain before selling his business for over $600k. Paul built his Amazon business in a very short amount of time and sold it at a huge profit, a profit he will use to give back. His aim in sharing his story is to never give up. Everyone is bound to face some uphill struggles at some point, but the goal is perseverance and pushing through until you reach the success you are looking to achieve.

Lucy's Success Story

The last story I would like to share with you is about a new mom who went from being broke and pregnant to being a millionaire through her Amazon FBA business. The amazing story of Lucy started back in 2017 when she started her business. She was expecting her second baby and had recently become a single parent. She took a course about selling on Amazon with money that she borrowed from her mom, and that gave her the motivation to start her business. Before taking the course, she had no experience in marketing or retail. She was a corporate lawyer in her previous job before leaving to spend time with her kids.

She had set a financial goal for herself of taking home $10,000 per month, which would mean that she needed to make $50,000 in sales, which she wanted to accomplish within two years. She did however reach this goal within seven months, which was absolutely amazing. Within 18 months, her Amazon business provided her with seven figures in sales, which in itself is a major accomplishment.

Her primary niche is baby products, and the products that she sells are what she personally uses, so she can promote them with confidence. Having experience and knowledge about the products she sells gives her an advantage because she can effectively communicate with her customers and speak through experience. Doing so has also helped her create great product listings and give excellent customer service.

She currently has 22 variations of one product and is working on another line of products. Although she uses Amazon as her primary vehicle for sales, she also has an Etsy shop and a website that she uses for her business. She believes that the ads you create should grab buyers' attention and give them a sense that you are telling a story.

She drives sales to her Amazon store through PPC campaigns, and most of her website visits come from Facebook and Instagram ads. She primarily uses Instagram for her ads and suggests that new business owners focus on using only one to two social media sites for promoting their businesses. This is because utilizing too many social media platforms can become overwhelming. Once your business is showing a profit, you can employ people to help manage other social media platforms.

In closing, this wonderfully successful entrepreneur would like to tell anyone who is looking to start an Amazon business to go for it. The skills that you need to start your business can be learned from various sources that are available to you. You need to believe that you can achieve success, and only then will you truly become successful.

Lucy's story is proof that with hard work, the right mindset, and education, anything is possible, and you can build a successful Amazon FBA business and achieve the financial freedom you are so desperately looking for.

Fact Box:
Throughout this chapter, I covered the following:

- Why customers are more likely to buy from social media.
- Amazon FBA trends you should know of.
- Strategies you can use to grow your Amazon FBA business.
- How to keep track of negative reviews.
- Holding yourself accountable.
- How to start your Amazon FBA business.
- Success stories from Amazon FBA business owners.

Segue: Now that we have reached the end of the final chapter, I would like to encourage you to read the conclusion, which provides a summary of everything I covered throughout this book.

Knowledge Is Power...

Let's Share It!

Now that you're well on your way to becoming a successful Amazon FBA business owner, you're in a perfect position to help someone else.

Simply by leaving your honest opinion of this book on Amazon, you'll show new readers where they can find the information they need to get their idea off the ground. And remember, more competition is only going to be good for business.

Thank you for your support. Everyone needs a helping hand in the beginning, and I'm thankful you're willing to reach out with yours.

>>> Click here to leave your review on Amazon.

Conclusion

Now that you have reached the end of this book, I would like to take the time to summarize everything that was covered in each chapter.

Chapter 1 covered a complete overview of what Amazon FBA is and how it works. I also covered the fees associated with Amazon FBA, as well as the advantages and disadvantages, so you can have a full understanding of what to expect. You also learned about why it's worth it to start a business using this model and how much you can expect to earn from your business.

Throughout Chapter 2 I covered the topic of registering your business and when it becomes necessary to do so. I provided you with the most important considerations that you need to keep in mind when choosing the right business structure and which one is best for your Amazon FBA business. You also learned about how to register your business in the U.S. in six easy steps. The last section of this chapter discussed the tax considerations you should keep in mind and what you should look out for.

In Chapter 3, you saw everything you should look out for when starting your Amazon FBA business, including the fees associated with it. I also covered how you can create your seller's account and provided a checklist that you can use to ensure that you add all the necessary information to your account.

Chapter 4 discussed the importance of finding the right products for your Amazon store. The various product categories on Amazon were also discussed, along with the most popular products for sale right now. Brands that should be avoided were also covered in this chapter.

Chapter 5 discussed how you should create the perfect listing to help your products sell more effectively. You also learned about optimizing your product listings and what you should look out for.

Throughout Chapter 6, I provided you with tips about drawing traffic to your shop. I also explained what exactly traffic is and how it is recorded in your store. You were also taught how to draw traffic to your shop from other sites to optimize your sales even further. This chapter also talked about how to improve your organic ranking by performing thorough keyword research.

In Chapter 7, we covered reviews and the importance of getting positive ones. I also discussed Amazon's rules concerning reviews and why buying reviews is never a good idea. You also saw how you can get great reviews from verified users to increase the possibility of your products being sold.

The final chapter discussed how you can grow your business even further and what trends you should be aware of. You were also provided with valuable strategies that you can implement in your business to ensure growth. Finally, I gave you success stories from entrepreneurs who have been able to not only start their businesses but also receive passive income from them.

In closing, I would like to take the opportunity to thank you for getting this far. I truly hope you enjoyed reading this book and you learned everything you need to know about starting your own profitable Amazon FBA business. I would like to ask you to leave a rating and a review of this book and your experience reading it. You can also let me know what you would like to read about next so I can continue providing you with informative books that will provide you with even more valuable tips and tricks.

Glossary

A+ Content: A program provided by Amazon that allows you to create more detailed product descriptions and add additional images, videos, and text to your listings.

A9: Search engine development and search advertising technology are run through this subsidiary. A9 helps to power Amazon's product search pages along with those of other e-commerce retailers.

A/B Testing: Also referred to as "split testing." This method is used to test two various websites or product listings to compare sales metrics. This is done through conversion rates, and it can increase your profits by around 25%.

Account Health: These are targets and policies set out by Amazon that sellers need to adhere to in order to continue selling on Amazon. These include customer service performance, product policy compliance, and shipping performance. You need to always keep your account health in mind when asking for product reviews.

Advertising Cost of Sales (ACoS): This is the percentage of sales that you may be spending on advertising.

Ad Daily Budget: This is the amount you are willing to spend on advertising daily.

Ad Impressions: The number of times your ad is viewed by individuals.

Ad Orders: The average number of times that customers click on your ads and then place an order.

Ad Sales: The average number of times customers click on your ads and then make a purchase.

Ad Spend: The amount you have spent on advertising sponsored campaigns.

Ad Status: The status of your ad group—your ads could be in the following states: running, paused, ended, archived, scheduled, incomplete, out of budget, or payment failure.

Ad Targeting: This is when you choose to select your own keywords for your ads or give Amazon permission to choose keywords on your behalf.

Affiliate Marketing: Affiliate marketing is the practice of paying individuals or external websites a commission for sales generated by using your link. Amazon has an affiliate program that can be signed up for in order to build a business.

Amazon Prime: A subscription service that provides users with access to various benefits. One of these benefits includes free 2-day shipping.

Amazon's Choice: When listings have a certain rating, price, and availability, you will receive a badge. You will see an increase in sales if you have this badge next to your listing.

Amazon Seller Central (ASC): In order to list, maintain, and view the performance of your products, you need to use this portal.

API (Application Programmer or Programming Interface): A code allowing two or more platforms or programs to connect with each other.

ASIN: Amazon Standard Identification Number. For each listing in your catalog, you will have a unique tracking identifier. This number is exclusive to Amazon.

A-to-Z Guarantee: A guarantee given by Amazon to buyers that the quality of products provided by sellers is high and that delivery will be done in a timely manner. The A-to-Z guarantee allows customers to make claims against sellers.

Automatic Targeted Ads: You don't need to add specific keywords when using this advertising model because Amazon will place ads to target relevant searches using specific terms.

B2B (Business-to-Business): This is when business is conducted between two companies. You may be able to qualify to sell directly to businesses instead of just selling to individuals.

Best-Seller Rank (BSR): Also referred to as the Amazon Seller Rank. This ranking is based on your current and historical sales data for every product you sell. This ranking can change frequently and is dynamic. Your BSR shows how your product has performed in the past and over the past few weeks. In order to track the performance of your products, his number should be tracked frequently.

Bid+: You would need to look for the highest-ranking keyword in your niche as an Amazon seller. You are able to use the Bid+ button to help you find these when running manual Amazon campaigns.

BOGO (Buy One Get One): These promotions are used when sellers launch new products on Amazon. In a nutshell, it is giving one product in exchange for the purchase of another. This strategy can also be used to persuade customers to make different purchases.

Brand: When you register your product under a specific name, you are creating a brand. You need to learn some advanced product research strategies in order to build a solid brand.

Brand Registry (BR): When registering your private label, your products will show up under the brand registry. This will protect your product against fraud and counterfeiting. You will also have access to the Product Display Ads and the Enhanced Brand Content features.

Buy Box: You will get large "Add to Cart" and "Buy Now" buttons when you qualify for Buy Box. This feature can help you increase sales especially if you are selling the same product as others.

Cost of Goods Sold (COGS): The total cost related to creating the product or service you will be selling. This amount includes material costs, packaging, shipping, duty taxes, etc.

Click Through Rate (CTR): The frequency of how often your ads are clicked on and how popular your product is will be displayed under this metric.

Conversion Rate (CR): The conversion rate is a phrase used to refer a customer to complete a number of actions like "Add to Cart" or completing a purchase.

Cost-per-Mil/Thousand/Impression (CPM/CPI): Another advertising method where you pay every time 1,000 individuals view your ads.

Coupons: To encourage clients to buy your products without running promotions, you can use Amazon's coupon program to offer discounts to your clients on your products.

Crowdfunding: Raising funds by contacting a large number of people.

Customs Clearance: When items move through an official department and collect and administer duties set out by the government for imported goods.

Delivery Duty Paid (DDP): The delivery and carriage of goods is the responsibility of the supplier; this requires applicable tariffs and duties to be paid.

Drop Shipping: Drop shipping is a business model where you are able to sell products without having to worry about shipping or keeping inventory. The responsibility of manufacturing, stocking inventory, and shipping your product will fall on the manufacturer.

Duty Tax: When importing or exporting goods, you will need to pay duty taxes as levied by the government.

Early Reviewer Program (EAN): A program that encourages buyers to leave an authentic review after purchasing a product, whether it's a one or five-star review.

Enhanced Brand Content (EBC): This feature gives you the opportunity to add a more detailed description of your product as well as add more images to your listings.

Export: When products are shipped outside of your country of residence.

FNSKU: Fulfillment Network Stock Keeping Unit. This is how Amazon tracks products that are unique to you that have been sent to an Amazon warehouse. A unique identifier is given to every product that passes through an Amazon warehouse.

Free Shipping Promo: You are able to provide your clients with this Amazon promotion for a limited time to boost sales.

Freight Forwarder: This service can help you communicate with your supplier regarding the coordination of your shipping details.

Fulfillment by Amazon (FBA): A feature by Amazon where you send products to an Amazon warehouse and they are then responsible for packing and shipping your products to customers on your behalf.

Fulfillment by Merchant (FBM): You will be completely responsible for the packing and shipping of products when using this model. You will also be handling any and all complaints related to your products.

Fulfillment Center (FC): This is where products are delivered before being shipped to customers who have made a purchase.

Fulfillment Fee: This is a fee charged by Amazon for the picking, packing, and shipping of your products through the platform.

Fourth Quarter: This is the last three months of the year, when sales often increase.

Gated Category: A category of products that are restricted to sellers and have not received approval from Amazon.

Ungated Category: A category of products that don't need approval by Amazon.

Giveaway Promo: Another promotion that you can offer to clients in order to increase your sales and your social media following or create a buzz around your brand.

GTIN (Global Trade Item Number): A number used as an identifier to look up information for various products.

Import: Shipping products from another country to the country in which you would like to sell them.

Invoice: A document sent to a buyer during a sales transaction indicating the product, quantity, and price of the products provided by you.

Landing Page: The section of a website that a link takes you to. This is often the home page of a specific website.

Lead Magnet: The practice of offering a product for free or at a discount in exchange for the contact details of a client, usually a phone number or email address.

Lightning Deals: These are limited-time deals offered by Amazon where sellers can set a discount on products and how long these deals will be available.

Listing: Your listing is the page where your product and all its information will be displayed for customers to see.

Long Tail Keywords: These are keywords that contain more than two words and are typically used when a specific niche is focused on.

Manually Targeted Ads: These are ad campaigns where you can choose the keywords you would like to use in your listings.

Minimum Advertising Price (MAP): When dealing with wholesalers or purchasing products directly from manufacturers, this may come up. This is to ensure that you are not selling products for the sale price or less than the manufacturer's.

Minimum Order Quantity (MOQ): This number is set out by a manufacturer or merchant and gives you an indication of how many products you need to order at once.

Manufacturer's Suggested Retail Price (MSRP): Manufacturers or merchants may, from time to time, suggest a price that you can sell products for.

Multi-Country Inventory (MCI): You are able to tell Amazon which countries you would like to sell your products to, and Amazon will then fulfill orders from your local fulfillment center.

MWS (Amazon's Marketplace Web Service): You are able to gain access to your API and MWS keys through this service (application programming interface).

Negative Keywords: Negative keywords are not always bad. These are words that you don't want on your listing when running Pay-per-Click ads because they may send your listing to the wrong searches. For example, adding the word "dog toy" to your plush dog toy means that it's intended for kids and not dogs.

Net Profit: This is the profit before COGS has been deducted.

Online Arbitrage: When sourcing products from one online e-commerce platform and then selling them on another platform for a profit.

Original Equipment Manufacturer (OEM): A company producing specific parts or equipment used by another manufacturer to market.

Performance Notification: This feature gives you information about how you are performing in terms of customer satisfaction.

Private Label: This process is when you sell products under your own brand and work directly with manufacturers to produce your product.

Pay-per-Click (PPC): Every time a buyer clicks on your Sponsored Product, Sponsored Brand, and Product Display Ad, you will be charged a fee. This feature is extremely popular with Amazon sellers.

Profit Margin: This is the amount that a seller earns after the COGS has been subtracted.

Promotions: In order to promote social media growth and increase sales, Amazon will offer a series of discounts and giveaways to their sellers.

Retail Arbitrage: This is when a seller finds underpriced products at retail stores and then sells them on Amazon for a profit.

Return on Investment (ROI): This is the amount that an investment either gains or loses over time. To calculate your ROI, you can use the following formula: ROI = (gain from the investment - the cost of investment) / cost of investment.

Sales Page: A web page created in an attempt to convince customers to purchase your products.

Sample: Products sent to you from manufacturers, suppliers, or wholesalers to show the quality, service, and competence of manufacturing.

Seller Central (SC): The page on Amazon that only sellers have access to and which is used to manage your account.

Search Engine Optimization (SEO): In order to increase the discoverability and organic search ranking of your product, you should put the most relevant, highly-searched keywords into your listings.

Stock Keeping Unit (SKU): These codes are used to identify specific products. These codes vary from supplier to supplier. They are used to keep track of inventory.

Sponsored Ads: Another feature of Pay-per-Click ads that gives you the opportunity to promote your products using keyword-targeted ads, which increases your visibility on Amazon.

Sponsored Brands: Sellers who are registered under the Amazon Brand Registry are given the opportunity to use this advertising feature on Amazon. Your brand and products will be promoted through a banner at the top, sides, and bottom of search result pages.

Sponsored Products: This advertising option lets your listing appear above other non-sponsored products and is the most popular advertising option.

Storefront: This is a feature that Amazon offers to sellers that enables them to create a store on Amazon and offer their customers an immersive virtual shopping experience. You are able to scale your business if you create an effective storefront.

Verified Reviews: A verified review is a review left by a customer who has purchased your product. A verified review carries more weight on Amazon.

Virtual Private Network (VPN): An encryption technology that gives information the ability to be moved across less secure connections.

Unverified Reviews: An unverified review is a review left by a customer who has not yet purchased the product they are reviewing. They carry less weight on Amazon, and that is why sellers should get reviews without being incentivized.

Universal Product Code (UPC): Similar to an SKU, this code is used to identify specific products and track information about them.

Upsell: The practice of convincing customers to purchase upgrades on their products or buy more expensive products in an attempt to make a profitable sale.

White Label (WL): White labels and private labels are very similar with one key difference. White labeling is the practice of removing your brand or label from one of your products in exchange for placing the label of another company on the product.

Wholesale Arbitrage: Wholesaling is another method of selling on Amazon and it is the practice of buying products in bulk at a discount and selling it for a profit on Amazon.

More Books From

The <u>MONEY</u>

<u>MAKING SERIES</u>

Optimize Your Profits And Go
From Side Hustle To Passive
Income With Minimal Effort

MONEY SNACKS

How To Start A Profitable Vending Machine Business In 5 Weeks

MONEY HOSTS

How To Start A Profitable Airbnb Business In 4 Weeks

MONEY BOOKS

How To Start A Profitable Self-
Publishing Business
In 21 Weeks

References

Amazon Brand. (2021, March 3). *10 Amazon Product Listing Optimization Tips.* Www.extensiv.com. https://www.extensiv.com/blog/amazon-listings

Amazon Selling Tips: New Account Setup + Strategies. (n.d.). BigCommerce. https://www.bigcommerce.com/articles/omnichannel-retail/amazon-selling-tips/

amazon.com *Website Traffic, Ranking, Analytics [December 2022]. (n.d.).* Semrush. https://www.semrush.com/website/amazon.com/overview/

Amazon.com. Inc. (2022, November 1). *What Is Amazon Stock's 2023 Forecast? Profitability And Buybacks.* SeekingAlpha. https://seekingalpha.com/article/4551475-what-is-amazon-stocks-2023-forecast

Barnes, J. (2020, September 24). *How We Built a 7 Figure Amazon FBA Business in 12*

Months. Your Lifestyle Business. https://yourlifestylebusiness.com/amazon-fba/

BigCommerce. (2020, June 6). *What is Website Traffic and how to interpret it to make....* BigCommerce. https://www.bigcommerce.com/ecommerce-answers/what-is-website-traffic-and-how-to-interpret-it/

Breslin+, S. (2019, December 11). *7 Ways You Can Grow Your Amazon FBA Business in 2023.* RepricerExpress. https://www.repricerexpress.com/grow-amazon-fba-business/

Chevalier, S. (2022, July 27). *Amazon marketplace active sellers by country.* Statista. https://www.statista.com/statistics/1086664/amazon-3p-seller-by-country/

Chi, N. (2022, May 4). *From Air Force to 7-Figure Amazon FBA Entrepreneur in Less Than 2 Years: Reggie Young's Story.* Empireflippers.com. https://empireflippers.com/air-force-to-amazon-entrepreneur/

Clearads. (2020, June 2). *The Importance of External Traffic to Amazon Product Listings and How to Do It* - ClearAds. https://www.clearads.co.uk/the-importance-of-external-traffic-to-amazon-products/

Competition quotes. (n.d.). *Quotefancy: Wallpapers With Inspirational Quotes.* https://quotefancy.com/competition-quotes

Connolly, A. (2023, February 5). *How Much Money Do Amazon Sellers Make?* Jungle Scout. https://www.junglescout.com/blog/how-much-money-amazon-sellers-make/

Connolly, B. (2021, December 8). *Do You Need an LLC to Sell on Amazon.* https://www.junglescout.com/blog/do-you-need-llc-to-sell-on-amazon/

Connolly, B. (2022a, February 25). *How to Handle Amazon Quantity Limits in 2022.* Jungle Scout. https://www.junglescout.com/blog/amazon-quantity-limits/

Connolly, B. (2022b, February 25). *How to Handle Amazon Quantity Limits in 2022.*

Jungle Scout.
https://www.junglescout.com/blog/amaz
on-quantity-limits/

Connolly, B. (2023a, January 12). *Taxes for
Amazon Sellers: Everything You Need to
Know (But Were Afraid to Ask).*
https://www.junglescout.com/blog/amaz
on-fba-taxes/

Connolly, B. (2023b, February 1). *How to Create
an Amazon Seller Account in 2022.*
Jungle Scout.
https://www.junglescout.com/blog/amaz
on-seller-registration-create-account/

Content Team. (2021, December 23). *Best
Business Entity Types For Amazon FBA:
How To Decide?* BBCIncorp - Offshore.
https://bbcincorp.com/offshore/articles/
best-business-entity-types-for-amazon-
fba

DataFeedWatch. (n.d.). *What are Amazon
Product Listings?*
Www.datafeedwatch.com.
https://www.datafeedwatch.com/academ
y/amazon-product-listings

Dayton, E. (2019a, February 8). 10 Fascinating
Amazon Statistics Sellers Need To Know

in 2019. The BigCommerce Blog.
https://www.bigcommerce.com/blog/am
azon-statistics/

Dayton, E. (2019b, February 8). *10 Fascinating Amazon Statistics Sellers Need To Know in 2019*. The BigCommerce Blog.
https://www.bigcommerce.com/blog/am
azon-statistics/

Dragan, L. (2016, May 13). *Let's Talk About Amazon Reviews: How We Spot the Fakes. Wirecutter: Reviews for the Real World.*
https://www.nytimes.com/wirecutter/blo
g/lets-talk-about-amazon-reviews/

Dunne, C. (2016, September 26). *5 Most Profitable Product Categories for Amazon FBA Sellers*. RepricerExpress.
https://www.repricerexpress.com/5-
profitable-product-categories-amazon-
fba/

Evensen, A. (2019, October 7). *Success Story: How I Built a 7-figure Amazon business with a $300 credit card.*
Www.profitguru.com.
https://www.profitguru.com/blog/succes
s-stories/7-figure-amazon-business

5 Reasons Amazon FBA Is Worth It in 2022. (n.d.). Forum. https://www.forumbrands.com/blog/5-reasons-amazon-fba-is-worth-it-in-2021

Hamrick, D. (2022, November 15). *Amazon Predictions 2020: 5 Big Changes to Look for in the New Year.* Jungle Scout. https://www.junglescout.com/blog/amazon-predictions/

Helium 10 Software. (2022, August 25). *How Many Sellers Are on Amazon?* Helium 10. https://www.helium10.com/blog/how-many-sellers-on-amazon/

How to Name a Business: Steps to Take + Guidelines. (n.d.). BigCommerce. https://www.bigcommerce.com/articles/ecommerce/how-to-name-a-business/

James, S. (2021, June 15). *Millionaire Amazon FBA Success Story (This Single Mom Makes 7-Figures).* Project Life Mastery. https://projectlifemastery.com/millionaire-amazon-fba-success-story/

Kevin. (2022, May 2). *How To Drive Traffic To Your Amazon Store? Here Are 3 Proven Tips That Work.* Zonbase.

https://www.zonbase.com/blog/how-to-drive-traffic-to-your-amazon-store/

Kulach, K. (2022, August 3). *Top selling items on Amazon in 2021: what to sell online right now*. Webinterpret. https://www.webinterpret.com/us/blog/top-selling-items-amazon/

Loiselle, M. (2021a). *3 Important Statistics That Show How Reviews Influence Consumers*. Dixa. https://www.dixa.com/blog/3-important-statistics-that-show-how-reviews-influence-consumers/

Loiselle, M. (2021b). *3 Important Statistics That Show How Reviews Influence Consumers*. Dixa. https://www.dixa.com/blog/3-important-statistics-that-show-how-reviews-influence-consumers/

Marrs, M. (2022, October 24). *5 Ways to Get 5-Star Amazon Customer Reviews*. Wordstream.com. https://www.wordstream.com/blog/ws/2014/04/10/amazon-reviews

McCormick, K. (n.d.). *9 Surprising Reasons It's Important for Businesses to Have*

Competitors. LocaliQ. https://localiq.com/blog/why-is-it-important-companies-have-competitors/

McDaniel, D. (2022a, May 17). *How to Sell on Amazon*. ManageByStats. https://managebystats.com/blog.how-to-sell-on-amazon

McDaniel, D. (2022b, May 17). *How to Sell on Amazon*. ManageByStats. https://managebystats.com/blog.how-to-sell-on-amazon

Mehlman, S. (2022, August 21). *How to Get Amazon Reviews: A Step-by-Step Guide*. https://www.similarweb.com/blog/ecom merce/amazon-insights/how-to-get-amazon-reviews/

Miller, K. (2022). *5 Reasons Amazon FBA Is Worth It in 2022*. Forum. https://www.forumbrands.com/blog/5-reasons-amazon-fba-is-worth-it-in-2021

N, A. (2023, January 3). *What is Amazon FBA and How Does It Work?* SellerApp. https://www.sellerapp.com/blog/amazon-fba-guide/

Omar. (2022a, August 14). *How Much Can You Make Selling on Amazon in 2023?* OJ Digital Solutions. https://ojdigitalsolutions.com/how-much-can-you-make-selling-on-amazon/#How-Much-Do-Beginner-Amazon-Sellers-Make

Omar. (2022b, August 14). *How Much Can You Make Selling on Amazon in 2023?* Digital Solutions. https://ojdigitalsolutions.com/how-much-can-you-make-selling-on-amazon/

Rise. (2018, April 24). *12 Inspiring Quotes to Help Small Business Owners.* Rise. https://risepeople.com/blog/quotes-for-small-business-owners/

Salvania, M. (2022, February 19). *Things Every Beginner Should Know When Starting Amazon FBA.* Seller Interactive. https://sellerinteractive.com/blog/when-starting-an-amazon-fba/

Seller Success Stories | *Finding success selling on Amazon.* (n.d.). Https://Sell.amazon.in. https://sell.amazon.in/seller-success-stories

Semrush. (n.d.). amazon.com *Website Traffic, Ranking, Analytics* [December 2022]. Semrush. Retrieved January 26, 2023, from https://www.semrush.com/website/amazon.com/overview/

The Helium 10 Software. (2022, January 14). *How Many Sellers Are on Amazon?* Helium 10. https://www.helium10.com/blog/how-many-sellers-on-amazon/

The Value Pendulum. (2022, November 1). *What Is Amazon Stock's 2023 Forecast? Profitability And Buybacks.* SeekingAlpha. https://seekingalpha.com/article/4551475-what-is-amazon-stocks-2023-forecast

Ugino, M. (2018, February 27). *Creating a Unique Amazon Product Listing: A Step-by-Step Guide.* Sellbrite. https://www.sellbrite.com/blog/amazon-listing-template/

Wawok, E. (2023, February 26). *How To Choose the Best Products for Amazon FBA — Listing Mirror.* Www.listingmirror.com.

https://www.listingmirror.com/choose-best-products-amazon-fba/

Wilder, C. (2023, February 21). *20 UNIQUE Amazon Business Opportunities to Start in 2023*. Niche Pursuits. https://www.nichepursuits.com/amazon-business-opportunities

Zelvis, N. (2022, April 15). *How to Register a Business in the US in 6 Easy Steps*. Management.org. https://management.org/business-registration

Made in the USA
Coppell, TX
25 September 2024

37728861R00128